Published 2012.
Pedigree Books Limited, Beech Hill House, Walnut Gardens, Exeter, Devon EX4 4DH
www.pedigreebooks.com | books@pedigreegroup.co.uk
The Pedigree trademark, email and website addresses, are the sole and exclusive properties of Pedigree Group Limited, used under licence in this publication.

Compiled and edited by Tim Rumball
Designed by Kim Hall
Sub-edited by Graham Clarke
Additional writing by Sally Charrett, Marc Rosenberg, Julia Heaton, Kris Collins
and Michelle Wheeler

Special thanks to the readers and contributors of *Amateur Gardening* magazine, who have assisted with the c ompilation of this Year Book.

All of the photographs in this book are © IPC Media Ltd, except the following: p6 pink 'Maid Marion' rose (David Austin Roses); p7 Superstock; P11 cloud-pruned box (Sandtex) and delphinium (Rob Keenan); p18 snowdrops in the green (GAP); p30 forsythia (GAP); p31 forsythia hedge (GAP); p34 ladybird (Wikimedia Commons); p36-38 all (Julia Phillips); p30 Tulip 'Yokahama' (Julia Phillips); p30 Tulip 'White Triumphator' (IFBC); p41 bird box (RSPB); p44 rose 'Teasing Georgia' (David Austin Roses); p52 Narcissus 'Pinza' (GAP); p53 layered bulbs (GWI); p66 cutting sweet peas (GAP); p68-71 (Peter Chatterton); p74 beetroot 'Alto', 'Chioggi Pink' and 'Burpees Gold' (Thompson & Morgan); p75 small soil test (Dave Bevan); p86 wisteria large (Getty Imgaes); p86 wisteria small (Marianne Majerus); p97 Cytisus 'La Coquette' (Graham Clarke); p98-101 (Susie White); p104 winter squash 'Harrier' (Thompson & Morgan); p116-117 Neil Ross; p120 spring cabbage (Dobies); p121 common wasp (Dave Bevan); p125 handweeding (Dave Bevan); p126-129 (Jacqui Hurst); p137 fruit picker tool (Darlac); p141 both pictures (GAP); p144 potato sacks (Dave Bevan); p156-159 (Naomi Slade); p167 both pictures (Dave Bevan); p170 Prunus 'Autumnalis Rosea' (GAP); p171 both pictures (Marianne Majerus); p172 tulips (RHS); p178 mistletoe berries (Wikipedia); p178 sowing mistletoe (GWI); p179 both pictures (Lucinda Costello); p184 (Alamy); p185 and p186 illustrations (Paper Rhino Illustrations).

contents

Amateur Gardening
Introduction

AMATEUR GARDENING is a weekly magazine for people who enjoy growing all types of ornamental and flowering garden plants, as well as fruit and vegetables. It is written and presented to be clear and easy to follow – it's also fun, because that's what gardening should be.

In this annual we've assembled material from across the seasons to give you information on a full gardening year.

Gardening means different things to different people – some want to create a beautiful garden like a work of art, with carefully designed and built hard landscaping, and a thoughtfully selected range of plants to complete the picture; others simply get pleasure from sowing a seed and, through their care, seeing it develop into a mature plant; and there are yet more who want to grow fruit and vegetables so they can enjoy really fresh harvests of varieties you'll never find in the supermarkets. We try to help people with all of their gardening aspirations. Gardening can be as simple or as complicated as you want to make it. Buy a tray of pansies and plant them in the flower bed, or just in a pot, water and deadhead them to keep the display fresh, and suddenly you're a gardener. Plant two or more different species and you've moved up a step to be a landscape designer, as you're having to make choices about positioning plants to look their best. From these humble beginnings, the sky's the limit. Even revered gardeners such as Christopher Lloyd, Gertrude Jekyll and Alan Titchmarsh started like this.

The aim of this book is to give you a hand to get the best from the plants you choose to grow, and to help you avoid some of the pitfalls. We've covered a broad range of subjects, so you can follow the story from start to finish through the year, or just dip in and take the bits you want!

■ **Amateur Gardening** is the UK's best selling weekly gardening magazine, and the oldest, launched in 1884. Published by IPC Media it sells around 40,000 copies through the news trade and subscriptions. It leads on practical gardening information that's clearly illustrated. It's award-winning gardening news pages regularly break major stories; expert columnists include **Bob Flowerdew** and **Anne Swithinbank** from *Gardeners' Question Time*; and former *Gardeners' World* presenters **Toby Buckland** and **Peter Seabrook** – Peter is also *The Sun* newspaper's Gardening Editor.
AG is on sale every Tuesday. For more detail, visit
www.amateurgardening.com

10 great flowers to get you growing

If you've never grown flowering plants before, try these easy-growing beauties which perform reliably and need no great skill

1 SNOWDROPS

■ START THE FLOWERING season early with the delightful late winter bloomer, *Galanthus nivalis*. Small and subtle but always sensational, the white petals with green or sometimes yellow flashes stand through snow, rain and wind to welcome the coming spring. Once the bulbs are established, clumps increase each year, needing little attention, and they're ideal tucked at the foot of deciduous shrubs or alongside larger perennials that die down over winter. Buy pots of snowdrops in leaf to plant out.

2 CROCUSES

■ THESE BULBS are the first to bring rich colour to our gardens in spring. You'll find everything from yellow, white, pale blue and pink-flowered species and varieties, through to the classic rich purples and blues – some even have striped petals. They are sold as bulbs in garden centres from late summer. Take care to buy the right types, as you can buy autumn flowering crocus, too. These are also easy to establish, but the flowers are more delicate and do best in a sheltered spot.

3 DAFFODILS

■ KEEP THE COLOUR coming as spring advances with daffodils. They can be planted in groups in garden borders, or in large containers, or 'naturalised' in lawns. The vibrant yellow flowers of traditional trumpet daffs are resilient and will stand through wind, rain and even snow to remind you of the increasingly sunny weather that should be just around the corner. Easy to plant, they're long-lasting and reliable. And if you really get hooked, there are lots of different varieties – some even scented!

4 SWEET PEAS

■ SPEAKING OF SCENT, if you start climbing sweet peas from seed in the autumn you can enjoy the honey-fragranced, brightly coloured flowers from late the following May. They do best grown up wigwams of canes in rich, deep garden soil, but they can be grown in large pots – just don't forget to water them. Sow batches of seeds in autumn, mid-winter and mid-spring for a continual blooms. Pick the flowers every day – if they set seed they'll stop flowering.

5 SUNFLOWERS

■ FOR SOME GARDENERS sunflowers are all about size – either the height of varieties like 'Mongolian Giant' which can reach 14ft (3.2m) tall, or the huge heads of 'Giant Single' that can grow to 30in (75cm) across. But modern varieties produce branching rather than single stemmed plants which have multiple flowers in a range of yellows, reds, browns and oranges – stunning as a feature plant in any garden border. Like sweet peas, they're hardy annuals and dead easy to grow.

6 TENDER GERANIUMS

■ AS SUMMER matures and the heat builds up, few flowers evoke sunny Mediterranean holidays like the tender geranium, or pelargonium. In pots around the patio, or used as bedding in flower borders, pelargoniums will keep belting out blooms through scorching weather. They're pretty drought-tolerant so if you're a forgetful waterer, they're ideal for you! Flowers are red, pink or white depending on variety. Buy plug plants in spring and grow them on under cover for pots or the border – it's cheaper!

7 OSTEOSPERMUMS

■ ANOTHER SUN worshiper, the osteospermum won't open its buds in the shade. But give it a scorched spot with free-draining soil, and it'll blast out masses of its daisy shaped flowers, each 2in (5cm) across, relentlessly. You'll find varieties that flower in pinks, purples, lilacs or yellow. In warm regions osteospermums will overwinter outdoors and perform for many years. In areas with cold winters, grow it in a good sized pot plunged in the soil, lift in autumn and overwinter in a frost-free greenhouse.

8 SWAN RIVER DAISIES

■ THIS DAISY-FLOWERED beauty extends the colour choice into whites and blues, and they're scented, too. This cottage garden classic is grown as an annual, raised from seeds sown in late February in a greenhouse – or buy plants from the garden centre in spring. Planted in a sunny border each low-growing plant will spread to about 24in (60cm). Water occasionally and pick off flowers that have gone over, and it'll flower until the first frosts.

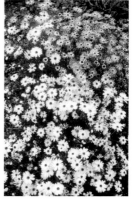

9 AFRICAN MARIGOLDS

■ THERE ARE FEW flowering plants that are easier to grow and reward with such a glorious display of big, yellow blooms. Perfect for bedding displays, and a real eye-catcher in containers on the patio, African marigolds (*Tagetes erecta*) are bigger, bolder and more verdant than French marigolds. Sow seeds in cell trays and set out young 'plug' plants in groups of three or five, in rich, moist soil for an amazing blast of yellow to orange colour.

10 DAHLIAS

■ VARIETY, LONGEVITY, simplicity and amazing good looks – that's dahlias for you. These tuberous-rooted perennials are such garden favourites they've been bred in thousands of shapes and colours. Garden centres will offer a limited range, but enough to keep the average gardener happy. Buy young plants if you lack gardening confidence, or save cash and buy the potato-like tubers to plant in pots for moving into the borders once sprouted. Lifted and protected from frost over winter, plants will last for many years.

JANUARY 2013

TUESDAY

1

WEDNESDAY

2

THURSDAY

3

FRIDAY

4

SATURDAY

5

SUNDAY

6

MONDAY

7

TUESDAY

8

Tools to get you started

A WELL-STOCKED shed can be built up over time. Write out a tool wish list and ask friends and relatives to buy them for you for Christmas and birthdays. However there are a few things you'll need to get started:

Spade
■ For planting and preparing or moving soils.

Fork
■ For breaking up soil during planting preparations.

Hand fork & trowel
■ Essential for planting, weeding and loosening soil around plants.

Rake
■ Levels the soil surface and breaks down lumps to produce a fine tilth. A spring tine rake with thin tines is used on lawns for collecting up leaves and grass cuttings.

Hoe
■ Chops down young weeds and breaks the soil surface around plants. Use weekly to keep on top of annual weeds. Various styles are available – try them to find one that suits you.

Secateurs
■ To cut stems and branches of woody plants up to pencil thickness. Also good for deadheading (removing spent flowers).

Watering can
■ Essential for watering pots and containers and settling in new plantings. Opt for changeable rose-end or sprinkler heads – a fine spray is used for seedlings, and a heavier spray for general watering.

Shears & loppers
■ Use long handled loppers for cutting woody stems up to 1in (2.5cm) thick. Shears are essential for clipping hedging and shaping plants.

Gloves
■ Keep hands clean, and free from scratches and scrapes, with a quality pair of garden-specific gloves.

Lawn mower
■ If you have a lawn you will have to mow it. For an average small to medium sized lawn, an electric mower is ideal.

JANUARY 2013

WEDNESDAY

9

THURSDAY

10

FRIDAY

11

SATURDAY

12

SUNDAY

13

MONDAY

14

TUESDAY

15

WEDNESDAY

16

Getting to know your plants

MOST PLANTS fall into two groups – woody and herbaceous. These are then split into sub-groups. Knowing these groups helps to make the right choice when stocking the garden.

Woody plants

■ These are plants with hard, woody stems (usually trees and shrubs). Most sold in this country are hardy enough to survive the British winter.

Shrubs and trees are differentiated by their growing habit. Shrubs have multiple stems, while trees have just one stem at ground level.

They both fall into two sub-groups – deciduous and evergreen. Deciduous plants, including acers, roses and hydrangeas lose their leaves ahead of winter. Evergreen plants including conifers and camellias, stay in leaf all year round.

Herbaceous plants

■ Plants with softer, non-woody stems, which tend to die back each winter

Annuals

■ Plants that germinate, flower and die off in one season. This group includes a wide range of flowers, vegetables, and herbs. These are great plants to start with as they offer quick results.

Hardy annuals (HA) such as sunflowers, sweet peas and nasturtiums can be sown outside in spring and/or autumn. Half hardy annuals (HHA), including petunias and begonias are frost-tender and must be started and grown on in heat until after the frosts.

Biennials

■ Plants that sprout and put on foliage growth in their first year, then flower and die in their second year. Examples include pansy and foxglove. Most biennials are hardy and can be sown in early summer, grown on in pots and then planted out in autumn to flower the following spring or summer.

Perennials

■ These are plants that grow for three years or more. This covers a wide range of plant types, from bulbs and miniature rockery alpines to towering border plants including delphiniums and verbascum.

Hardy perennials (HP) can be planted out to live in the garden for many years. Half hardy perennials (HHP) like fuchsia and pelargonium will not survive freezing conditions.

JANUARY 2013

THURSDAY

17

FRIDAY

18

SATURDAY

19

SUNDAY

20

MONDAY

21

TUESDAY

22

WEDNESDAY

23

THURSDAY

24

Which compost to use

A WIDE RANGE of composts is available for different gardening jobs. Here's a guide to what each of the common types is used for:

Multi-purpose composts
■ Usually a mixture of peat and recycled green waste with some fertiliser added. Some contain loam (fine, nutrient-rich soil).
Uses: Sowing, potting on, seasonal pots, veg growing, improving soils.
Advice: Best for one season's use in pots. For long-term pots use soil-based compost.

Soil-based composts
■ Many soil-based composts are John Innes formulae, which is made up of sterilised loam with smaller amounts of peat and sand added. Varying amounts of fertiliser are added depending on the use: JI No1 is used for potting up seedlings and young plants (small amount of fertiliser). JI No2 is used for potting on young plants and bulbs (twice the amount of fertiliser) and JI No3 is used for potting up mature plants (three times the amount of fertiliser).

Ericaceous composts
■ Peat and soil-based formulations available for growing acid-loving (ericaceous) plants such as camellias and heathers, in pots.
Advice: Grow ericaceous plants in pots if your garden soil is chalky.

Seed and cuttings compost
■ Fine-grade compost, often with added sand and perlite.
Uses: Seed sowing and taking cuttings.
Advice: Seedlings and cuttings need potting on into richer compost as soon as they are well rooted.

Peat-free composts
■ An eco-friendly compost. Ingredients include coir (coconut fibre), pine bark, and composted garden waste.
Advice: Some say these composts perform poorly.

Potting composts
■ Soil-based, peat-based or peat-free formulations are available for potting up well established plants.
Advice: Potting mixes tend to have higher feed levels of fertiliser included, which are needed by large plants.

Specialist composts
■ Some plants need types of growing media (or 'compost') with very particular nutrient and/or drainage qualities.
Advice: Orchids, bonsai, cacti and carnivorous plants are just a few groups that need special compost blends.

JANUARY 2013

FRIDAY

25

SATURDAY

26

SUNDAY

27

MONDAY

28

TUESDAY

29

WEDNESDAY

30

THURSDAY

31

Sprays to tackle pests and diseases

C HEMICAL AND ORGANIC sprays can help us in our battle against garden pests and diseases. Before using them, always read the label and follow the instructions.

Insecticides to tackle pests

■ There are two basic types of insecticide for tackling small garden pests. Contact insecticides must be sprayed onto the pest, while systemic insecticides enter the sap stream of the plant and poison pests that eat the leaves. Systemic insecticides include Bug Clear Ultra, Plant Rescue Bug Killer and Provado Ultimate Bug Killer.

Most sprays have pictures of the bugs they control on their packaging. Some sprays are only suitable for ornamental plants. If you want to use insecticide on the veg patch, buy one that says it's suitable for use on fruit & veg.

Fungicides to tackle diseases

■ Many sprays for controlling fungal diseases such as mildew, rust and mould are now systemic as opposed to contact in action.

The most commonly available systemic sprays such as Fungus Fighter Disease Control, Plant Rescue Fungus Control and FungusClear can be applied at the first sign of a problem.

They all tackle a wide range of fungal infections including mildew, grey mould, rust and blackspot, and give long-lasting control.

Herbicides to tackle weeds

■ There are three different kinds of herbicide for dealing with weeds and unwanted plants. Contact weedkillers only kill off the parts of the plant they are applied to. They are great for annual weeds but will not deal with deep-rooting perennial weeds.

Systemic weedkillers (absorbed into the sap stream) include RoundUp, Tough Rootkill and Tumbleweed, all based on the chemical glyphosate. They enter the sap stream to kill foliage and deep roots, but they don't persist and contaminate the soil.

Residual weedkillers such as Ground Clear stay in the soil for months and kill all plants. They are intended for use on paths and driveways where no plants grow. Never apply residual weedkillers to the garden soil.

Designing a garden

If it's too cold to work outside, use the time inside to design the garden of your dreams

MOST OF us want our gardens to have a particular look, but it can be a real challenge to get that look just right. The best way is to start the process is with a strong plan in mind – and winter is the ideal time to put that plan together. So get out your tape measure, some pencils and a pad, spread out the seed and nursery catalogues, and get planning!

Think logically:

■ IF, FOR example, you want a patio for entertaining on summer evenings, site it where you'll enjoy the end-of-day sunshine.

Spacing:

■ SPACE PLANTS out carefully. If you set plants too close to each other you'll only have to move them in a year or two. And if you set them too far apart you'll have a gappy border – or left-over plants.

Mixing colours:

■ THE 'COLOUR WHEEL' (here represented in the shape of a flower) shows how colours can compliment or contrast with each other. Those close to each other provide harmony, while opposites contrast. A mix of colours thrown together to create a 'fruit salad' look needs foliage to harmonise things.

Dividing space:

■ MAKE A list of the elements you want, work out how much space you want to give over to each, and set them out on paper. Link the elements – lawn, raised beds, veg plot, storage shed, etc. – with pathways to create a flow through the space.

Be strict:

■ IF WORKING with an established garden it seems a shame to get rid of plants, but if they don't fit your plans they are weeds – get rid of them.

Illusion of space:

■ CREATE A deep border to 'push back' the fence or hedge line. Grade it with small plants at the front and taller plants at the back. This will make the bed seem bigger than it is in reality.

Blending:

■ BLUR BOUNDARIES of adjacent areas around the garden by mixing the edges. For example, between natural and formal areas use a mix of wild and cultivated plant varieties.

Single colour themes:

■ COLOUR CREATES the mood of a garden. To make colours work well, you should give the space a sense of depth and interest in other ways, such as with height, size and even the texture of plants.

Design tips for effective borders

■ BEFORE YOU buy any plants, make a plan. Don't just plonk a row of same-height or same-species plants in a long line along the fence! With a good mix of plants in mind, adopt the 'triangle rule' – a tip from Alan Titchmarsh. Use a pencil to draw a series of faint triangles on a straight line. Overlap them and use different sizes and angles.

Then create a front-on view of your border by filling in the triangles with the mature shapes of your chosen plants – most good catalogues and plant labels will give you an idea of mature sizes.

Directly below the line, draw out a bird's eye view of the bed or border, and mark out the plant locations – rub out the triangles and an instant border appears.

Reds and yellows are energising and warming, looking great on the dullest of days. Used at the back of the garden they have the effect of bringing the border forward.

Cooling blue and white flowering plants have the opposite effect – great on hot sunny days – and a great contrast to hot colours, making that part of the border appear to recede.

Creating an interesting layout using the lawn as your guide

1 This basic design creates little interest in the garden, but do not discount it if play space for children is an important factor in your garden's design.

2 Narrowing borders towards the back will shorten overall perspective. Grading plants, shortest at the front, tallest at the back, will enhance this.

3 Curving the lawn to one side of the garden will change the flow, and channel the eye to a given focal point. It also allows for deeper border planting areas.

4 Bringing the border into the lawn and planting it with tall plants will enable you to create a hidden area and encourage exploration of the space.

5 A meandering lawn slows the pace of a design and leads the eye slowly to the back of the garden adding scope and interest to border plantings.

6 This design incorporates both meandering curves in the lawn and a hidden space behind the border to bring a natural, organic feel to the garden.

Illustrations: Kris Collins

Anne's Family Garden

Pots from the winter plot

Looking ahead to the warmer months, **Anne** springs into action and plants up a low-cost container that will provide colour and interest all year round

AT THIS time of year we are all longing for spring to arrive. But gardeners have it sorted. We can actually see things stirring in the garden, including winter aconites and snowdrops. Buds are congregating at the crowns of Lenten hellebores, and *Daphne odora* is already opening its fragrant blooms.

With all this growth and optimism in the air, I decided to plant up a container while spending almost nothing. We inherited some big pots from my late aunt's garden, and as I'm always propagating plants there's usually a small nursery of young plants clustered around the outside of the greenhouse.

A well-stocked garden takes on a life of its own, and as long as you don't weed too assiduously, will yield plenty of interesting seedlings and suckers.

Needing a tall specimen plant for the middle of the pot, I tracked down and lifted out an attractive evergreen *Euphorbia characias* that had set itself in the exotic border. A good shrubby type, it has its origins in Portugal, and parts of the western Mediterranean. This was soon joined by a hardy cranesbill, *Geranium peloponnesiacum* (bought last summer on a whim from the garden shop at Killerton House near Exeter), and some perennial wallflowers.

"A well-stocked garden takes on a life of its own"

Frond memories

While weeding a year or so ago I found and potted a number of fern sporelings. They have turned into good little plants. So I selected what looked like soft shield ferns (*Polystichum setiferum*) and alternated them with the only plants bought in especially for the job. These are some slightly forced *Iris* 'Katherine Hodgkin', a beautiful yet subtle Reticulata iris with pale blue, gold and lilac markings.

Containers are indispensable for gardeners with tiny plots where there are no soil beds. But even when you have plenty of space there are often large areas of paving or driveway to soften.

I like the idea of using perennials in pots as, looked after well, they should last almost indefinitely. And we'll enjoy colour and interest all year round from this pot.

Perfect posies

Another way of enjoying the garden, and lifting spirits, is to pick sprigs of winter flowers and foliage to fill posy vases. I always start off thinking I won't find anything and end up being surprised by just how much the winter garden has to offer. My recent trawl of the borders delivered white heather, pink *Viburnum farreri*, *Pittosporum* 'Irene Paterson', hebe, fragrant winter honeysuckle, rose hips and periwinkle.

Step by step
Planting a perennial pot

FILL
I placed pot shards over the drain holes and added compost (50:50 soilless and John Innes No2), then in went the euphorbia, geranium and erysimums.

ARRANGE
Plants were arranged and brought to the right height by adding or taking away compost under their roots. Next to go in were ferns that grew in the garden from spores.

FINISH
Finally some Iris 'Katherine Hodgkin' were added. These should come up again next year. Gaps were filled with compost and the plants were all then given a good watering.

Your gardening week

Spring's a comin'!

The snowdrop is the perfect flower to raise winter spirits, says **Anna Toeman**

In the Victorian language of flowers the snowdrop means hope

IN THE language of flowers, that dialect so beloved of the Victorians, the snowdrop stands for consolation and hope – and these sentiments couldn't have been attached to a more deserving plant! They are among the first flowers to appear in the New Year and bring with them the promise that spring is on its way.

Snowdrops, with their pendulous white flowers carried singly on short stems, are instantly recognisable. Although all quite similar, each of the 19 species can be distinguished from the other by a combination of features – size, leaf colour and flowering time, as well as those green markings.

But there are more than 1000 named cultivars, and many differ only by the slightest variation in their markings. Often, only an expert can determine which cultivar is which, and these passionate connoisseurs are collectively known as "galanthophiles"

For the best results, buy and plant snowdrops when they are 'in the green' which means just after the flowers fade and while the leaves are still green

There are several species of snowdrop you may encounter in the garden, but the one that carpets woodland valleys in February is the English or common snowdrop, *Galanthus nivalis.*

Its history is uncertain but whether it is a native, a garden escapee, or a hybrid of both, it is widely naturalised across parts of Britain. It has been shown that many of the largest wild colonies are closely associated with Church land where the bulbs were planted as a symbol of purity.

The history of the Crimean snowdrop – *G. plicatus* – is much better known. British soldiers during the Crimean War brought bulbs back home to plant because they had been so uplifted by the sight of this flower when it appeared in swathes across ravaged battlefields. This species is larger than our common snowdrop, reaching up to 10in (25cm) in flower.

Giant snowdrop

It will be no surprise to learn that the giant snowdrop, *G. elwesii*, is so called due to its relatively large flowers. It reaches just 4-6in (10-15cm) tall but each flower is up to 1¼in (3cm) long. Deliciously honey-scented, the inner petals are almost entirely covered by large markings; the grey-green leaves are broad and sometimes twisted.

It would be an impossible task to begin to describe the hundreds of cultivars but some are easy to grow and widely available. 'S. Arnott' is well regarded with its flowers that boast a strong honey scent and have an inverted "V" at the tip of each inner petal; 'Magnet' is similar, but the flowers are smaller and not so strongly scented, and the margins of the young leaves roll backwards.

DETAIL DOUBLE FLOWER:
Some snowdrop species have amazing double flowers. This is Galanthus dionysus

How to grow

■ THE TRICK in growing snowdrops is to get them established – once you've succeeded, they need little attention. Snowdrops do best in humus-rich, heavy loam with plenty of moisture, even in summer – conditions that replicate their natural woodland habitat. They grow well beneath deciduous shrubs and trees (in soil or grass), in the rockeries and even in containers, and can cope well with competition as long as their leaves receive plenty of light.

To establish bulbs it is essential to keep them moist, and the best way to do this is to plant them 'in the green' – after flowering but while still in leaf.

SUPPLIERS

■ **Broadleigh Bulbs**
☎ 01823 286231
🖱 www.broadleighbulbs.co.uk

■ **Avon bulbs**
☎ 01460 242177
🖱 www.avonbulbs.co.uk

WHERE TO SEE SNOWDROPS

For a truly breathtaking snowdrop experience, visit one of the great snowdrop gardens, where you'll see them growing en masse:

CAMBO ESTATE GARDENS
(National Collection Holder), Kingsbarns, near St Andrews, Fife, KY16 8QD
☎ **(01333) 450313**
🖱 **www.cambosnowdrops.com**

COLESBOURNE PARK
Colesbourne, nr Cheltenham, Gloucestershire, GL53 9NP
☎ **(01242) 870264**
🖱 **www.snowdrop.org.uk**

EAST LAMBROOK MANOR
South Petherton, Somerset, TA13 5HH
☎ **(01460) 240328**
🖱 **www.eastlambrook.com**

Gardener's tea break

CROSSWORD...

just for fun Answers below

ACROSS

1 Clumps of small trees and shrubs growing naturally, or grass held together at the base (5)
3 Green or blackfly (5)
7 Prudish, and 4/7ths of a spring-flowering woodland genus (4)
8 It goes on the road when it's cold – or in pots to facilitate drainage (4)
9 With responsibility, one carries this – especially when watering! (3)
11 Tall men to visit the vegetable plots! (9) (anag)
14 Monty inclines his head up and down, to indicate agreement – backwards! (3)
16 Not a common thing (4)
17 To make these you chop a tree down, and then chop it up! (4)
18 Hard work propagating trees and shrubs by transplanting buds! (5)
19 Genus name for rhubarb (5)

DOWN

1 Part of a flower – but not a petal! (5) (anag)
2 Genus name for the 9 down imperial! (11)
4 *Cotoneaster horizontalis* is often referred to as the _____ cotoneaster! (11)
5 Fruits of the tropical *Phoenix dactylifera* palm (5)
6 Garden ones (*Pisum sativum*) are edible, but sweet ones (*Lathyrus odoratus*) are not! (3)
9 The ____ imperial is 2 down imperialis! (5)
10 A wanderer, as in the scented-leaved *Pelargonium* 'Lara _____' (5)
12 Small shoot or twig of a tree or other plant; a spray (5)
13 Broom made from a bundle of twigs tied onto a shaft (5)
15 *Avena sativa* – a widely cultivated cereal grass (3)

SPOT THE DIFFERENCE

The Alpine house at the Royal Horticultural Society's Wisley Garden in Surrey is always a riot of colour in the darkest, coldest days of winter. But can you spot the FOUR differences between these two pictures?
(Answers can be found at the bottom of the page)

WASTE NOT, WANT NOT   Mailbag

This sign, spotted while walking past a neighbour's garden, brought a smile to my face.
Charlotte Joseph, Lelant, Cornwall

SPUD SPACING

Q Owen Prentice asks: "I want to grow second early potatoes in a raised bed. I would like to know how much space I need to leave between each tuber, so that I know how many I need to purchase."

A Set your second earlies 15-18in (38-45cm) apart within the row, and set rows 27-30in (68-75cm) apart. The larger spacing will allow for bigger tubers. To allow enough room for all of the tubers to achieve optimum growth, the first and last tuber in each row need to be planted at half the recommended spacing from the edge of the bed – as do the first and last row.

Decorative garden

Your gardening week

Sowing sweet peas

Sweet peas add great colour and scent to gardens, and they're easy to grow from seed

SWEET PEAS are a sure-fire winner in our gardens. They give scent, colour and (certainly with the tall, climbing varieties) height and structure.

Seeds can be sown in September/October to overwinter in a cold frame, or January, February, March and April.

A late spring sowing is advisable in very cold areas. Autumn sown plants may flower earlier, but only by a week or two.

Sweet pea seeds have a hard coat, which some gardeners try to soften ahead of sowing, either by soaking or cutting away a sliver of seed coating, but it is not essential, providing you use good quality, fresh seeds.

There are many varieties to choose from, and your decision will depend on the colour you want and the space you have. Some varieties don't have much scent – read the packet.

Some varieties are bred to do well in pots and hanging baskets – they're bushier and do not get so high: great for patios or small gardens.

Seedling aftercare

■ Stand pots of autumn sown seedlings in an unheated greenhouse or cold frame over winter, keeping compost moist. Protect from mice, slugs, heavy rain and severe frosts. Plants should withstand temperatures of -6°C (21°F).

When the plants are about 6in (15cm) tall and have three sets of leaves showing, pinch out the top of the plant above the second pair of leaves to encourage sideshoot growth for denser plants. Plant out in early spring as soon as the ground is dry, and warm enough to work with.

SIMPLE STEPS TO SWEET PEA SUCCESS

1

■ Threequarters fill your containers – which should be around 6in (15cm) deep – with multipurpose compost, and water well. Then top up with dry compost.

2

■ Make sowing holes with a thick pen or dibber. Set the seed ¾in (2cm) deep, and lightly cover. Do not water again until most of the seeds have germinated.

3

■ Cover the containers with newspaper and set in an unheated greenhouse or cold frame. Remove paper at the first sign of germination, normally in 7-10 days.

Your gardening week

Sow early veg crops

Start tomatoes, peppers and aubergines now for growing under glass

SOWING THESE tender crops in January, and again in March, will give harvests from early June from the greenhouse, and from the later sowing through summer outdoors to the first frosts – or later if you keep them in a frost-free greenhouse or conservatory.

Warmth is essential for January sowing, so a heated propagator or mat will be called for. Sowing temperatures for these crops range between 18-23°C (64-73°F).

Light also plays an important factor. If you're sowing your seed in the house, keep the pots on a south-facing windowsill that lets in plenty of natural light. Without good light plants can become leggy, producing too much stem between leaf nodes, causing weakness and possible collapse later in the season.

You can sow seeds in a variety of ways. Several seeds into one 3in (7.5cm) pot, or sow two per cell in cell trays. Alternatively sow a whole packet across an open tray of compost (though you probably won't want that many plants!). As long as the receptacle fits in the propagator, the choice is yours. Here we're using Haxnick's root trainers (www.haxnicks.co.uk) for strong rootball development, and sowing two seeds per pod in case one fails. If two germinate we'll pick off the weaker one. All three crops can be treated as described below.

Step by step

How to make an early sowing of tomatoes, peppers and aubergines
You'll need: Seed trays, pots or root trainers; compost, vermiculite and a heated propagator

1 Fill trays, pots or root trainers with a fine seed and cutting compost. Firm down lightly and water well, then let the container drain for a minute

2 Sow your seed evenly in an open tray or two seeds per cell, or five seeds per 3in (7cm) pot. Cover with a fine layer of compost or vermiculite

3 Place in a heated propagator at 18-23°C (64-73°F). Keep vents closed until seeds sprout to keep a high humidity. Ventilate immediately seeds germinate

4 When pot/tray sown seedlings are large enough to handle, pot up individually into 3in (7.5cm) pots of multipurpose compost, water and keep warm

Quick tips
January
...more things to do

1 Hit the sales

■ HIGH STREET stores aren't the only places to find a bargain in the January sales. Visit garden centres and DIY stores early in the month to make the most of their discounted offerings. Spending now will save you useful amounts of money later in the year.

2 Grit paths & driveways

■ KEEP THE postie happy this winter and grit paths and drives to prevent them icing over. Check and reapply after heavy rain as this can wash your efforts away.

3 Deal with the Christmas tree

■ RATHER THAN take your Christmas tree to the recycling centre, turn it into a useful soil conditioner. The acidic properties of pine needles are a great soil improver for ericaceous plants such as azaleas, rhododendrons and blueberries. Run branches through a shredder and add chippings to ericaceous beds.

4 Plan the veg plot

■ GET OUT on the veg plot now to plan this year's crop rotations. Leafy brassicas should grow where peas and beans grew last year. Peas and beans should go where potatoes were grown, and put your spuds where the root veg and onions grew last year.

5 Snow patrol

■ KNOCK HEAVY snowfall from tree and shrub branches to prevent them snapping under the extra weight. Also remove snow from shed and greenhouse roofs.

6 Force rhubarb

■ TWO YEAR old and older rhubarb can be forced for early stems by placing a forcing pot or black bin over them to exclude light. After six or seven weeks pale pink stems will be ripe for picking.

7 Sow sweet peas

■ JANUARY IS a good time to start off seeds of sweet peas. Set trays or pots of seed on a warm windowsill. As soon as the majority of seedlings emerge, place trays and pots in a frost-free greenhouse or cold frame. They will put on slow growth ready for spring planting.

FEBRUARY 2013

FRIDAY

1

SATURDAY

2

SUNDAY

3

MONDAY

4

TUESDAY

5

WEDNESDAY

6

THURSDAY

7

FRIDAY

8

Seed catalogues

Buying seeds mail order from catalogues has certain advantages for the gardener

PLANT AND seed catalogues are a wonderful resource for the keen gardener. They provide access to a much larger range of varieties than you'll find in any garden centre, and you can select what you want at leisure, and order by post or telephone.

The plants and seeds will be delivered to your door, so the small fee you pay for postage covers what you'd spend travelling to the garden centre. The suppliers are specialists so the quality is generally high and the product will be supplied with clear care instructions. And all of the seed catalogue suppliers introduce new varieties each year.

Bulk discounting

Ordering in bulk often attracts discounts and special offers which you're unlikely to get at garden centres. Winter is the perfect time to browse catalogues, plan your garden and decide what you're going to grow, then order seeds for sowing in spring to stock your borders for the year ahead.

Almost every seed catalogue will be supported by a website, so with a computer you can source useful information about the plants in their range, browse the company's offerings online, and maybe order that way, too.

Here are contact numbers for some of the many popular seed catalogue suppliers:

Suttons Seeds
✆ 0844 922 0606 🖰 www.suttons.co.uk

DT Brown
✆ 0845 371 0532 🖰 www.dtbrownseeds.co.uk

Kings Seeds
✆ 01376 570000
🖰 www.kingsseeds.com

Mr Fothergills
✆ 0845 371 0518
🖰 www.mr-fothergills.co.uk

Thompson & Morgan
✆ 0844 573 1818
🖰 www.thompson-morgan.com

FEBRUARY 2013

SATURDAY

9

SUNDAY

10

MONDAY

11

TUESDAY

12

WEDNESDAY

13

THURSDAY

14

FRIDAY

15

SATURDAY

16

Chitting seed potatoes

START EARLY varieties of seed potatoes now for planting out next month under cloches. Chitting, or pre-sprouting them helps them to produce an earlier crop. It's not worth chitting maincrop varieties as these need a long growing season. When choosing your seed potatoes pick tubers that are about the size of an egg, evenly-sized, and plump – not shrivelled. Also look for the ones with lots of elliptical shaped eyes (dormant buds) on them.

QUICK TIP
If you don't have any egg boxes to hand, use modular seed trays to stand your spuds in

Frost-free windowsill

Egg boxes are great for standing seed potatoes in to chit, because the seed tubers are roughly egg-sized, and sit securely in each cell. Place each tuber so the end with the most eyes is up in the air. Then put the box on a cool, well-lit, frost-free window sill.

The buds will start to produce shoots after about two weeks. Once these shoots reach 1-2in (2.5-5cm) long, the seed potatoes are ready to be planted. Traditionally, plant potatoes outdoors on St. Patrick's Day (March 17), or later if harsh weather persists. However, if you warm the soil with a plastic cloche for a couple of weeks, then plant beneath the cloche, the plants should be fine. Or plant them in sacks or pots in a sheltered spot.

FEBRUARY 2013

SUNDAY
17

MONDAY
18

TUESDAY
19

WEDNESDAY
20

THURSDAY
21

FRIDAY
22

SATURDAY
23

SUNDAY
24

Sowing seeds of flowering plants

YOU CAN start sowing seeds of flowering plants in heated propagators from late February onwards, providing you can keep the young plants protected from frosts and in good light until the weather warms up outside. A greenhouse is ideal. A large cloche will be OK, and at a pinch you can raise a few early plants on a good bright windowsill indoors.

Step by step ➤ Sowing seeds

1 Fill pots or trays with a good seed compost. Remove bumps and hollows by lightly pressing and levelling the surface for even sowing.

2 Evenly water with a fine-rosed watering can. The finer the spray, the less disturbance to the compost. Allow to fully drain before sowing.

3 Sow seed evenly across the surface, then cover with a thin layer of compost or vermiculite. Label with tray or pot with seed name and date.

4 Place in a heated propagator or seal in an inflated clear plastic bag. Open vents, or remove bag, once the majority of seedlings have appeared.

5 Keep compost moist. When seedlings have their first set of true leaves, tease them out of the compost with a dibber or pencil, and pot up individually.

FEBRUARY 2013

MONDAY

25

TUESDAY

26

WEDNESDAY

27

THURSDAY

28

Buying 'plug plants'

Half-way between sowing seed and buying mature plants

PLUG PLANTS are for you if you don't want the bother of growing summer bedding, fruit and veg from seed. Plug plants are seedlings supplied in their own mini plug of soil. Temperatures of 16-18°C (60-65°F) are required so you will need a heated greenhouse or space indoors on a windowsill for success.

From mid-spring, garden centres offer the most popular lines of bedding plants, and some vegetables, as plug, but the choice is greater from online and mail order suppliers.

Step by step — Three steps to plug plant success

1 Lightly water your plug plants and leave them to drain. Fill cell trays or small pots with multi-purpose compost. Then use a dibber or thick pen to make a planting hole in each cell/pot.

2 Remove plug plants from their tray, pushing the dibber through drainage holes beneath the tray to release them, and place one in each planting hole, lightly firming in.

3 Label each tray or pot – it's easy to get them mixed up. Water with a fine rose watering can. Stand in a frost-free spot in good light. Pot on when roots appear through drainage holes.

Your gardening week

Winter digging

Improve the soil ready for planting – as long as it's neither frozen nor water-logged

IMPROVING THE soil is important before establishing any new garden bed, for flowers, fruit or vegetables. Good preparation at this stage can transform the performance of ornamental borders for years to come. It is essential to improve soil regularly when growing crops.

Digging and incorporating well rotted organic matter improves the soil structure and drainage, and it lets air in.

Soil structure is determined by how individual soil granules bind together, and the amount of air between them. Structure has a major influence on water and air movement through the soil, and affects seed germination and subsequent root growth.

Clay soils are made up of small particles with very little air between them. Sandy soils have lots of air between larger particles.

Some gardeners use a no-dig technique that depends on thick mulches. Others swear by digging. It is good exercise and gives the gardener a chance to see close-up what the soil is like.

The soil can be dug any time between autumn and early spring. The heavier (clay) your soil, the earlier it should be dug. Light soils should be done now.

Rotary tillers

■ Often called rotary cultivators, or 'rotavators' (a trade name), these petrol or electric motor powered tools can cover large areas quickly, but require a degree of skill and a fair amount of strength to use effectively. Some argue that rotavating spoils soil structure and does not go deep enough. But if you want to get a large or neglected plot into cultivation quickly, it may be the best option.

Always wear safety boots and other protective clothing when using tillers and rotary cultivators. With electric powered models, always work with the wire behind you.

Clay soil

■ Improving the structure of a clay soil will also improve drainage. Add organic matter such as well-rotted manure, garden compost or leaf mould. Single-dig this into the top 8-10in (20-25cm).

If you can roll your soil into a ball in your hand, it is clay

Sandy soil

■ Lots of added manure and garden compost dug in now and left over winter will improve the structure of sandy soil. It is possible to import heavier soil and to mix this in with a sandy soil, but this is very expensive so not usually done in gardens.

Sandy soil drains quickly and doesn't hold nutrients well

Double digging

■ Double digging is better for the soil than single digging. 'Double' simply means that organic matter is added to the soil further down (double the depth than that of single digging). Deep cultivation like this is of particular benefit to deeper-rooting plants, including trees and shrubs. It improves fertility exactly where the plant needs it– at the roots.

Here's how to do it:

1 Set a line along one edge of the area to be double-dug. Take out a trench along the line, one spade blade's depth, and place this soil into a wheelbarrow.

2 Using a garden fork, turn over the bottom of the trench, to de-compact the soil. At this stage remove any large stones, roots or other debris seen.

3 Place a thick layer of well-rotted manure or garden compost, or a good quality soil conditioner into the trench and fork it into the base.

4 Alongside the first trench start to dig another. Turn the soil from this trench into the first one, adding a little rotted manure or compost.

5 Repeat the process, working your way across the plot. The soil level will be raised, but it will sink down after rainfall.

6 When you've added the organic matter to the last trench, use the soil in the wheelbarrow to refill it. Let the soil settle for a month.

Single digging

■ This is the simplest form of digging
Here's how to do it:

1 Spread a 2-3in (5-7cm) deep layer of well rotted compost or manure over the entire area to be dug.

2 Mark a line along one edge of the area and, working backwards, dig a spit of soil with your spade and turn it back into the same hole, burying the compost.

3 Work backwards across the plot, turning at each end, until the whole area has been turned and the soil improver is incorporated into the top layer of soil back into the same hole burying the compost.

Blaze
of Glory

Careful pruning can transform the early spring flowering forsythia, says plantsman **Matthew Wilson**

The bright shocking-yellow flowers of forsythia are strongly associated with the end of winter and the beginning of spring

I WONDER how many of us, pushed to name a favourite spring-flowering shrub, would suggest the forsythia? Despite its many virtues – fast growing, tough, easy-to-cultivate and completely smothered in flowers when in bloom – forsythia seems to suffer from a major image problem, to the point that some gardeners actively loathe it. But if you concentrate on those virtues for a moment, surely it deserves a place alongside hamamelis (witch hazel) as a great early flowering shrub?

I suspect that some gardeners dislike the flower colour. Its brassy, vivid yellow blooms are definitely a 'Marmite' colour –

one that can be hard to place successfully alongside the other usually softer yellows of spring, such as daffodils and primroses. But equally culpable I'm sure, is the way in which forsythia gets used – or rather, abused – in the garden, for if ever there was a shrub that suffered from the worst excesses of hacking and chopping that a pair of secateurs, powered hedge trimmers and bow saw can administer, forsythia must surely be it.

Weeping habit

Most forsythia are native to parts of Asia (mainly China and Korea), with one species native to southern Europe. Two species (*F. viridissima* and *F. suspensa*) were introduced to the West and

Give forsythia enough space to allow its graceful stems to arch naturally, and leave a good 5ft (1.5m) around the rootball

For Matthew Wilson, forsythia just isn't quite right when it's tightly pruned – "those vivid yellow flowers look just a little bit odd when embedded in the rigid geometry of a hedge", he says

these are the parents of *Forsythia* x *intermedia* which, in varying forms, is what most of us grow in our gardens. I actually prefer *F. suspensa* to the hybrid forms, as it usually has a lovely, gracefully weeping habit and large golden yellow flowers, but it can be very variable in growth, and at 9ft (3m) tall is too big for most small gardens.

Forsythia grow rapidly, reaching maturity in comfortably under a decade. This fast and sometimes wayward growth is one of the reasons why they suffer from pruning butchery. But being vigorous by nature, the reaction of this shrub is simply to grow even more enthusiastically!

Forsythia is also a popular choice of plant for hedges, and this is one application where I join the loathers. For me it just isn't quite right as a hedge; not neat enough between trims to have the same qualities as yew, beech, hornbeam of even privet, and it is not loose enough to give it the natural look of a native hedge.

And those vivid yellow flowers just look a little bit odd embedded in the rigid geometry of a hedge.

But, well grown and correctly pruned, forsythia can be a real asset to the garden.

> **Forsythia are often subjected to pruning butchery**

GROWING FORSYTHIA WELL

■ GIVE THEM PLENTY OF SPACE. For popular forms like 'Lynwood Variety' this means allowing a circle at least 5ft (1.5m) around from the root ball to grow into. Pruning is really straightforward. Do it right after flowering – if you prune later you'll be removing the flowers for next year. After five or six years remove up to a third of the oldest stems completely, right down to the ground. A decent feed with garden compost or well-rotted manure, and a good drink of water if the conditions are dry, and that's about it.

Your gardening week

BELOW: Bob Flowerdew

ABOVE: Peter Seabrook

Experts offer advice on
pruning trees & shrubs

Learn how and when to prune your garden shrubs, say **Peter Seabrook** and **Bob Flowerdew**

FLOWERING SHRUBS have for some reason dropped out of the limelight in recent years, says **Peter Seabrook**. Fifty years ago young plants of ribes (flowering currant), forsythia (circled centre), potentilla, philadelphus (mock orange, pictured bottom right) and weigela were sold in their hundreds of thousands.

Container growing and garden centres popularised evergreens, which look more attractive from November to March, with the result that cheerful deciduous shrubs slipped down the charts. This is a pity because our suburban streets can be lit up with the sunshine yellow of massed forsythia blossom; potentillas flower continuously for weeks through the summer, while fragrant mock orange perfume hangs heavily on the air on warm summer evenings.

These shrubs can grow quickly, and the more vigorous ones can become too large for the available space in today's smaller gardens. Even so, they respond well to being regularly cut down to size.

Remember these general rules:
Several deciduous shrubs provide a good source of cut flowers, both forsythia and lilac being good examples. Dormant forsythia stems cut in February and brought indoors will soon open in a vase of water; doing this also keeps down over-vigorous growth.

When it comes to lilac, pruning out sizeable branches just as they come into flower will stimulate growth for large flower heads next year.

Cut stems in a vase will take up water better when all the leaves are removed, and some other foliage used as in-fill.

Most trees and shrubs provide height and structure to any planting scheme so while the branches are bare take a good look at your plot and see where the introduction of one or two will make for improvement. If funds are limited, a few hardwood cuttings (and a few years) is all it takes for the easiest kinds.

> **66 Forsythia stems cut now and brought indoors will open in a vase of water 99**

- ■ **EARLY FLOWERING** – prune after flowering (as for forsythia and ribes)
- ■ **SUMMER FLOWERING** – thin out old branches after flowering (philadelphus and lilac)
- ■ **LATE SUMMER/AUTUMN FLOWERING** – prune hard back in late winter (as with buddleja)

Above: bush roses can be massacred annually
Right: use a pruning saw to thin out congested shrubs

I THINK we tend to be a bit timid when it comes to pruning flowering shrubs, says **Bob Flowerdew**. It's best to leave them well alone generally – if they're doing a good job then don't bother them.

In the fruit garden, of course, the reverse is true: we are generally required to prune to ensure quality, size and regular crops. But most flowering shrubs give fair displays for years, even decades, with no annual pruning. Naturally they do get bigger, and somehow we don't notice slow deterioration of the overall flowering, year-by-year, until the blooming becomes obviously patchy or poor.

You can give most hardy shrubs a shearing over just as the flowers fade. It works, though it is much derided by 'experts' as 'producing a lollipop on a stick' – but it does appeal to me.

Sporadic pruning

However I'm lazy, and I tend to practice not annual, but sporadic pruning. When shrubs get too big I just cut most down really hard in late winter. Of course there are always a few that will die. Still, replacements are cheap.

The majority of shrubs respond magnificently, and usually with a mass of new shoots. I may thin these but often they do fine left alone. The shrubs bounce back and, re-invigorated, give tremendous shows over the next few years, often with huge leaves, bigger flowers and denser shows of bloom.

Of course this rush fades away and they settle down into their old ways over the following decade or so. Some, such as roses of course, and buddlejas, can even be massacred annually and, if well fed, give a far more impressive display of bigger blooms than older, unpruned bushes. But I view this as too much effort, unless I really want prize-winning displays.

Very slow-growing shrubs (such as *Daphne odora*) don't respond so well to serious cutting back, and are better pruned in a much more considered way. But just think of most plants generally used for hedging, and all their close relatives. Many are already known to respond well to this sort of treatment. And I suspect in practice it's what most of us do anyway.

> ❝ **The shrubs bounce back and give better shows, with huge leaves and bigger flowers** ❞

Daphne odora does not respond very well to pruning

Gardener's tea break

WORDSEARCH

T	D	I	U	M	R	A	I	D	W
N	I	E	L	K	G	B	H	O	E
A	Y	T	N	O	M	U	A	N	D
E	L	O	C	F	F	C	R	H	R
G	A	A	M	H	A	K	A	T	E
B	A	T	N	R	M	L	S	F	W
O	I	V	O	N	L	A	T	I	O
B	O	L	I	B	E	N	R	W	L
R	A	V	E	N	Y	D	N	S	F
L	E	H	C	A	R	E	O	J	H

This word search contains names of famous gardeners: these names are listed below, and in the grid they may be read across, backwards, up, down or diagonally. Letters may be shared between words. After the listed names are found there are 13 letters remaining; arrange these to make the KEYWORDS – the name of a another famous TV gardener – of his generation!

ALAN	FLOWERDEW	SARAH
ANNE	GAVIN	SWIFT
BOB	JOE	TITCHMARSH
BUCKLAND	KLEIN	TOBY
CAROL	MONTY	
DIARMUID	RACHEL	
DON	RAVEN	

MY CHRISTMAS TREE IS DYING

Q Diana Norris asks: "I bought a live Christmas tree (*Picea abies*) and potted it up after the festive season. The top seems to have died while other parts are beginning to sprout new growth. Will it survive?"

A It's common for some shoots to die off while others seem to be healthy. Refurbish your tree in spring by cutting back dead portions to live growth. Follow this by feeding with Miracle-Gro Plant Food weekly throughout spring and summer. Also water freely to keep the compost nicely moist, but not soggy. In time, when the tree's roots push through the holes in the bottom of the pot, reset it into a larger pot, 6in (15cm) greater in diameter. Firm a good ericaceous compost around the roots, and water it in well.

SPOT THE DIFFERENCE

BBC Radio 4's *Gardeners' Question Time* is the longest-running gardening show on the wireless, attracting over two million listeners every week. But can you spot the FOUR differences between these two pictures of the expert panellists (L-R Anne Swithinbank, Pippa Greenwood, Bob Flowerdew and chairman Eric Robson)? Answers can be found a the bottom of the page

PLEASE DON'T TAKE AWAY MY HOME!

Mailbag

AFTER TIDYING up plants every spring to make way for new growth, I'd put the clippings in bags to be collected by the council. I felt good that I was recycling and doing my bit. But I soon realised that I had hardly any ladybirds in my garden.

When the council offered a special deal on compost bins I bought two, and last year, after my usual spring clean up, I found six ladybirds crawling around in the bin. Previously I must have been gathering them up and sending them off to the council for recycling!
Mrs L Stevens, Broadstairs, Kent

SPOT THE DIFFERENCE In the lower picture the stripes on Pippa Greenwood's t-shirt have disappeared; Eric Robson's beard is darker; a post has appeared (bottom); and Bob Flowerdew's pony-tail has vanished.

WORDSEARCH KEYWORDS: **GEOFF HAMILTON**

Horticultural expert and former Gardeners' World TV presenter

The Classic Gardener

Peter Seabrook

If in doubt, don't weed!

Self-sown seedlings can provide free flowers every summer, says **Peter**

NATURE'S GIFTS, in the form of self-sown flowers, are a welcome addition to most gardens: they often grow much better in their own selected sites and look more natural there.

I love to see foxgloves (digitalis) growing randomly among shrubs, or honesty (lunaria) flowering in shaded corners from where the 'silver dollar' seed pods shine out in late autumn. Self-sown erigeron flowers profusely from cracks in paving along the base of walls. All of these, and many others, play a valuable part in garden decoration.

So you must learn to identify desirable seedlings when weeding beds and borders, and leave well alone. Many, with unique qualities, can in time become garden favourites.

Verbena 'Seabrook's Lavender' is a case in point. This was first spotted as a chance seedling, found flowering in my front border. It is now grown by many thousands of gardeners in Britain, and abroad.

Love-in-a-mist (nigella) takes some beating for its clear blue summer flowers and shapely seed pods – all from a modestly-priced packet of seeds. It is many years since I sowed packets of the mid- and dark-blue kinds – a good investment when their progeny can be enjoyed year on year. Self-sown seedlings of nigella, cornflower, calendula and cerinthe that

"Self-sown seed looks more natural in its own selected site"

germinated last autumn will provide the earliest flowers in my garden this summer. When the weather's mild, thick clumps of seedlings can be thinned out, and these thinning may be used to fill up spare spaces.

Transplants will come into flower a week or two later, which just extends the flowering season.

If you don't have these annual flowers then seeds sown in cell trays under glass will give you a flying start. Sow two or three seeds per cell, and thin down to one seedling after they are well established.

Allotmenteers should consider raising enough seedlings of, say, tall blue cornflower to plant across their plots. One row of seedlings spaced 6in (15cm) apart, and cut regularly, will produce many bunches of flowers through the summer.

When stems get too short to cut, they can be left to self-seed ready for next summer.

Great ideas Tips for more colourful flowers and marking seed beds

Look out for *Campanula* 'Blue Rivulet', a chance seedling spotted by Norfolk plantsman Adrian Bloom

Mix a little annual flax seed in with carrot seed to produce a decorative, flowering vegetable crop

Mix a little quick-germinating radish seed in with annuals sown outdoors, to mark where flowers will follow

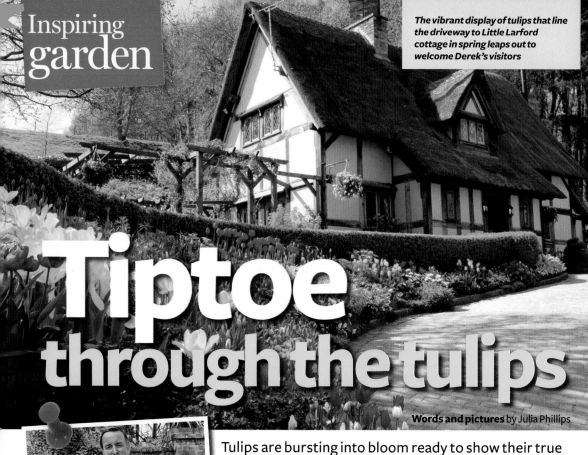

The vibrant display of tulips that line the driveway to Little Larford cottage in spring leaps out to welcome Derek's visitors

Tiptoe through the tulips

Words and pictures by Julia Phillips

Tulips are bursting into bloom ready to show their true colours in **Derek Walker's** Worcestershire garden

Garden notes

Name: Derek Walker

Address: Little Larford near Stourport on Severn, Worcestershire

Size of garden: Half acre terraced garden surrounding a picturesque thatched cottage

Soil type: Light, sandy and acid

Special features: Situated on a hillside overlooking the Severn Valley. Some 17,000 bulbs are planted in October to produce an outstanding display featuring 70 different varieties laid out in broad colour schemes through the borders.

Season visited: Spring

YOU CAN tiptoe through the tulips to your hearts content in one corner of rural Worcestershire. At Little Larford, Derek Walker has planted 17,000 bulbs and created a fanfare of colour – in praise of April.

It requires some forward planning to stage such a show of colour, so in October retired nurseryman Derek sets about planting thousands of bulbs in his half acre hill-top garden, not forgetting 50 or 60 pots and troughs. It takes him and a colleague just over a week to complete the task, planting up to 2,000 bulbs a day, many under-planted with pansies, primroses or polyanthus.

Then he just has to sit back and wait. The result is a dazzling assortment of colours and shapes as 70 varieties repeat throughout the garden emerging to colour the hillside terraces.

Derek had only been living at Little Larford for three years when he made the decision to hold his first Tulip Time for a National Gardens Scheme open day. "The reason for concentrating on tulips was because it was such a young garden and many of the plants weren't old enough to make an impact. So I decided to plant a mass of tulip bulbs for an instant display – after a long dull winter

it's nice to start the year with a splash of colour," he said.

Preparation of the soil seems to be the key to successful planting. A project like Tulip Time requires expertise, something Derek has plenty of as he has been in the horticultural business since the age of 17, starting with a small rented nursery.

By the time he retired Derek was supplying local authorities in the Midlands area with vast quantities of plants, grown in large glasshouses.

"I've never done anything else apart from gardening. My father was a gardener for a brewery and looked after pub gardens, hanging baskets and the like. So as soon as I left school I set up in the nursery business and never looked back!

"I missed it when I first retired but as I was always too busy for

"It is a heavy maintenance garden because after the tulips flower we take up all the bulbs and put in bedding plants for the summer. I grow all these in the greenhouse myself", said Derek. "I prepare for planting very thoroughly and then water everything I grow with a weak solution of Maxicrop, and Tomorite when they start to flower."

Preparation of the soil seems to be the key to successful planting, and getting the best from bulbs like Tulipa 'Orange Emperor'. Derek explained: "I put down a general fertiliser of fish, blood and bone three times a year: firstly in October, then again in May and then at the end of June. We have a light soil here so it's ideal for planting tulips."

Tulipa 'Orange Emperor' with red and white 'Lip Gloss' and double cream 'Mount Tacoma' blend beautifully together. "It's best to plant winter bedding and bulbs in mid-October. That way they get good growth before the hard frosts set in," said Derek.

"The garden is very peaceful and there is woodland and a mini bird sanctuary behind with up to 78 different wild birds visiting the area and breeding there."

my own garden this is the first time I have had time to really enjoy it".

Derek and his wife Lin had previously lived in a three acre property, and that's exactly what they instructed the estate agents to search for when they started looking for their new home.

"The brief also stated a requirement for a flat site so that we could have greenhouses," said Derek. "We ended up here on a hillside with only a 20ft x 10ft (6m x 3.1m) glasshouse!

"It was the thatched cottage, the position and the views over the valley that sold it to us.

"Our aim was to have a quiet life and spend more time at our holiday home, however we are now very busy indeed with the garden," said Derek. "We have planted everything and added the pergola walk, lawn and rhododendron border. Although it's work, it's all very enjoyable and there is plenty of time for sitting outside and enjoying the colour as well."

> **❝I missed it when I first retired but as I was always too busy for my own garden this is the first time I have had time to really enjoy it❞**

The pergola walk runs alongside a bowling lawn and is underplanted with polyanthus and Tulipa 'Peaches and Cream'. Since opening the garden there has never been a dull moment for Derek. He said: "I'm President of the local horticultural society. We have talks, go on visits and there are plenty of social activities including playing bowls on my lawn!"

There are hundreds of tulips to choose from, grouped by flower form, height and blooming time. This is 'Yokahama', which grows to 14in (35cm)

The colourful facts
about tulips

1 **THOUGH CLOSELY** associated with Holland, the tulip hails from Persia where the word means "turban"– describing the flower shape. During the 16th century they became so popular in Holland that it lead to 'Tulipomania', when people traded tulip bulbs for huge sums of money.

2 **IN GENERAL** the bigger the bulb, the bigger the bloom. Tulips also tend to loose quality but you can have satisfying results for quite a few years by fertilising the soil around plantings each season.

3 **REPLANT WITH** new bulbs every two to three years.

4 **OCTOBER OR** November is the ideal time for planting, but any time before the ground freezes will do.

5 **TULIPS WILL** bloom in almost any soil, anywhere. The only place where growing them will be a problem is in wet soil, as the bulbs can rot.

Above: 'White Triumphator' is a pure white hybrid tulip to 24in (60cm)
Below: 'Negrita' is one of the best plum-coloured tulips, to 20in (50cm)

Perfect for pots, 'Angelique' is pale pink, and grows to 18in (45cm)

Your gardening week

How to grow
potatoes

This crop is tasty, filling and good for you

POTATOES ARE PROBABLY the most popular vegetable in Britain. They are high in carbohydrate and get blamed for making us fat, but it's the way we prepare them (especially frying) that adds the most calories. Potatoes cooked without fat (and eaten with their skins on) offer calcium, iron, phosphorus and potassium as well as vitamins C, A, B and P.

Varieties to try

The **four main categories** of potato are early, second early, main crop (categorised by the length of time to maturity and time of harvest) and salad (second early or maincrop types with waxy flesh).

Popular types include **'Maris Bard'** (early); **'Charlotte'** (second early); **'King Edward'** and the red-skinned **'Desiree'** (maincrop); and **'Pink Fir Apple'** (maincrop salad).

SIMPLE STEPS

SITE & SOIL

■ IDEAL IS a deep soil which is rich in organic matter, and free draining. It should be neutral to acidic – limey soil promotes canker disease. Add garden compost or well rotted manure to soil in autumn before planting. Site should be sunny and open.

WHEN TO PLANT

■ PLANT SEED tubers in spring after 'chitting' or sprouting (top picture) early varieties by placing tubers on a bright windowsill for 2-3 weeks (see p25).

PLANT OUTDOORS

■ PLANT CHITTED tubers (centre picture) of earlies from March in warm areas; second earlies from mid-March; and maincrops from April. Set earlies 6in (15cm) deep and 12in (30cm) apart in rows 24in (60cm) apart. Set all others at the same depth but with a more generous 18in (45cm) between tubers and 30in (70cm) between rows. Mark rows clearly

PLANT IN CONTAINERS

■ HALF FILL a large pot or growing bag with potting compost, space 1-4 chitted tubers evenly over the surface, and cover with 2-3in (5-7.5cm) of compost. Water and put in a sheltered, sunny spot.

ROUTINE CARE

■ AS GREEN shoots appear, draw surrounding soil up around them, leaving tips showing (bottom picture). Repeat process 2-3 times as shoots grow. Add compost to container-grown plants as shoots grow, until container is full. Keep soil/compost moist.

HARVESTING

■ AFTER FLOWERING, check early varieties – scrape away soil/compost to see if tubers have formed. When you find them, lift a few plants with a fork, but give the rest 2-3 more weeks. Lift second earlies and maincrops when the tops start to die down.

Quick tips

February ...more things to do

1 Prepare for new lawns

■ SPRING IS ideal for sowing or laying a new lawn. If ground is not waterlogged or frozen, prepare soils in advance this month. Clear plants and weeds, dig over the area, tread flat and rake level. This will give the soil time to settle ahead of laying.

2 Warm soils for early sowing

■ COVER BARE soil with black plastic, newspaper or horticultural fleece to pre-warm the soil for earlier sowing. This will speed up germination for earlier crops or flowers. Or use a clear plastic to allow dormant weed seeds to kick into growth for easy removal.

3 Put up nest boxes

■ BIRDS RARELY choose a newly sited bird box. Install boxes now, well ahead of the breeding season, in secluded areas of the garden. Avoid having the entrance holes facing prevailing winds.

4 Feed soils

■ CHEMICAL FERTILISERS such as Growmore, and organic feeds such as chicken manure pellets, fish blood and bone, and bone meal are slow to release their goodness into border soils (six weeks or longer). Apply these now to soils ready for the growing season. Wait until late spring to apply faster acting options.

5 Long season chillies

■ IN THE warmth of a heated propagator you can start to make early sowings of your favourite chilli varieties. This will give you a longer season for earlier and more cropping. If there is space in the propagator, also sow tomatoes, peppers and aubergines.

6 Trim winter heathers

■ WINTER HEATHERS (*Erica carnea*) that have finished flowering can be trimmed back just below the spent flowers with shears or secateurs, to prevent woody growth and bare patches higher up the stems.

7 Instant bulb colour

■ IF YOU HAVE GAPS to fill in borders, or didn't plant dormant bulbs in autumn, get an instant colour fix with pre-sprouted, spring-flowering bulbs now. Garden centres have all manner of spring favourites (daffodils, crocuses, iris, snow drops etc) in small pots that can be planted straight out.

MARCH 2013

FRIDAY

1

SATURDAY

2

SUNDAY

3

MONDAY

4

TUESDAY

5

WEDNESDAY

6

THURSDAY

7

FRIDAY

8

Creating new borders
in the lawn

Step by step

1 Use a length of hose to mark the shape of your new bed or border. Work along this line with a half moon to cut into the turf to define the edges.

2 Use a spade to lift the turf from the area. If you have space, stack this turf upside down, soak and leave for six months to create quality loam.

3 Turn over the soil in your new bed using a border fork, spade or a tiller and remove any weed roots. Once turned, roughly level the soil with a rake.

4 Add soil conditioner to the area. Spent growbag compost is great for lightening heavy soils. Turn in, rake level, tread in, then again.

MARCH 2013

SATURDAY

9

SUNDAY

10

MONDAY

11

TUESDAY

12

WEDNESDAY

13

THURSDAY

14

FRIDAY

15

SATURDAY

16

Protect seedlings with
a garden frame

CLEAR PLASTIC- or glass-windowed 'coldframes' give enough protection from rain, wind and frost to allow young seedlings, cuttings and small plants to be overwintered. They can also be used to start off spring sowings a few weeks earlier compared to open ground sowing. They are also ideal for acclimatising greenhouse-raised young plants to outdoor temperatures – a process known as 'hardening off'.

Few coldframes are built much higher than 18in (45cm) however, so they will not easily allow overwintering of larger plants. Position so they face south, to make the most of the sun's warmth in winter.

Buy ready-made cold frames from garden centres and mail order suppliers. Or make a simple shelter by leaning an old glazed window against a south facing wall and tuck your plants behind it. Block the open sides. Water plants in your frame when necessary. Ventilate on warm days.

MARCH 2013

SUNDAY

17

MONDAY

18

TUESDAY

19

WEDNESDAY

20

THURSDAY

21

FRIDAY

22

SATURDAY

23

SUNDAY

24

Feed your roses

ROSES GROW vigorously and flower generously, so they need plenty of feeding. Applying a suitable granular fertiliser now will give time for it to work down to the roots to fuel spring growth.

First tidy up around the base of plants removing weeds and plant debris. Fork lightly through the surface of the soil with a hand fork to ease compaction in the top couple

of inches. Scatter a couple of handfuls of granular fertiliser around the base of each plant and rake it into the soil.

You can use a general balanced fertiliser such as Growmore, but a better option is a special rose fertiliser which is high in potassium to boost flower production. After applying the fertiliser water it in, especially if the

ground is dry – but not so heavily that you wash it all away!

End with a thick mulch of well rotted manure or garden compost around the base of each plant.

MARCH 2013

MONDAY
25

TUESDAY
26

WEDNESDAY
27

THURSDAY
28

FRIDAY
29

SATURDAY
30

SUNDAY
31

Service garden tools

MARCH USUALLY brings with it enough bad weather to keep gardeners off their plots for at least one weekend in the month. Use the time to go through all of your tools – cleaning, adjusting, sharpening and mending. Wipe over hand tools with a damp cloth removing caked-on soil, let them dry then rub exposed metal parts with a lightly oiled cloth.

Sharpen cutting edges (including your hoe) with a whetstone or one of the many sharpening tools now available from garden centres.

If you use a petrol lawnmower, get it serviced if necessary. Clean the blade housing area underneath rotary mowers, scraping off caked-on grass and earth. Check cutting blades on all mowers and sharpen or replace as necessary.

Check cables and plugs on electrical power tools for

fraying, breaks or cracks. Repair or replace. Stock up on fuel and oil for some power tools.

Wash and check over gardening gloves for tears or broken seams and replace if necessary.

All of this will ball ne time well spent!

Your gardening week

Planning a veg plot

Before sowing your veg for the year, think about the best use of space on your plot

THERE'S NOTHING like eating home grown produce. Even in the smallest of gardens there is room to add a few vegetables, whether you set aside a plot, or plant a few crops between ornamentals in a flower bed – cottage garden style.

But if you want regular, seasonal harvests it's best to set aside an area of the garden for dedicated vegetable, herb and fruit production.

And, for best results, forward planning is important. Success all comes down to moving crops around the plot, year by year – know as rotation – which spreads the demands on nutrients from the soil, and avoids build-up of pests and diseases.

Digging

■ DIG OVER the entire veg plot annually – preferably in autumn so winter frost action can help to break up clods of soil. Add well-rotted organic matter to improve soil structure and help to feed plants, by single or double digging (see p28)

Manuring

■ ADD MANURE whilst digging if the soil is 'hungry' (sandy and 'thin'). Well-rotted garden compost can be used instead. If the soil is fertile, and in a good condition, manure only the part of the plot to grow veg listed under '3' below. Avoid manuring before planting root crops.

Liming

■ ADD LIME if soil is neutral-to-acidic in nature; do a soil test to be sure. Apply before growing brassicas. Never add lime just before planting potatoes, and not at the same time as adding manure as this can cause a chemical reaction. Sprinkle lime over a plot rather than dig it in.

The three-year rotation

■ Simply take your plot and divide it into three equal parts. In the first year one of the following crop groups should be grown in each of the thirds. Each year following, the crop groups as indicated (right) should be moved into the next bed along:

1

GREENS
The cabbage family – broccoli, Brussels sprouts, cabbages, kale, cauliflowers and Oriental greens, as well as kohl rabi, radishes, swedes and turnips.

2

ROOT/TUBER CROPS
Beetroot, carrots, parsnips, Jerusalem artichokes and potatoes. These don't have a high need for nitrogen, so are good after brassicas.

3

OTHERS
Peas and beans, peppers, aubergines, peppers, tomatoes and sweet corn. Also the onion family, and leafy veg such as lettuce, spinach, celery and leaf beet.

Other rotation ideas

The FOUR-year crop rotation

■SOME GARDENERS prefer to adopt a four-year rotation regime. This is where the vegetable plot is divided into quarters, with each section moving on one place each year. In four- and five-year plans potatoes are not generally considered to be root crops. Therefore the most appropriate crops for the sections are as follows:

1st quarter: Brassicas
2nd quarter: Peas and beans (add manure)
3rd quarter: Potatoes and fruiting vegetables
4th quarter: The onion family and root veg

Above: Beetroot is a root crop
Bottom: Brussels sprouts are in the brassica family

The FIVE-year crop rotation

■EXPERT VEGETABLE growers (and experienced allotmenteers) often choose a five-year rotation. This is a regime that is definitely more suited to large kitchen gardens or an allotment. Arguably it is the best rotation plan, as it means that five years pass before any single crop is grown again in the same place. The plot is divided into fifths, each section moving on one place each year.

1st fifth: Brassicas
2nd fifth: Peas and beans (add manure)
3rd fifth: Potatoes and fruiting vegetables
4th fifth: The onion family
5th fifth: Root vegetables

Above: Runner beans like lots of manure in the soil
Below: Leeks are in the onion family

Greenhouse and conservatory plants like this Pandora are waking after their winter rest. Working out what to do with them next is good fun.

Getting into shape

Anne gives awakening plants some early season pruning to set them on their way

THERE'S A lot of pruning to do this month, and my first job was a straightforward cutting back of hardy fuchsia stems out in the garden. I'll trim them almost to the base, leaving short stubs behind, each holding nodes ready to burst forth into new growth, which will rise to around 5ft (1.5m) and flower in summer and autumn.

Fuchsia magellanica makes a fine seasonal flowering hedge along the kitchen garden fence in a damp, shady spot. Similar treatment will be meted out to sun-loving *Caryopteris clandonensis* whose stems re-grow to produce blue flowers against silvery grey foliage in late summer.

Under glass

Over-wintered greenhouse and conservatory plants need attention at this time too, and I brought some together in order to decide how to deal with them. Sometimes I like to work around the plants, snipping away small dead pieces and looking them over before I decide on a detailed course of action.

I was particularly sad to see that the variegated angel's trumpet (brugmansia) that I had left in the unheated greenhouse over winter had very soggy stems, and may have been frosted.

> *"Over-wintered greenhouse and conservatory plants need attention too"*

At least I took no chance with the lovely climbing bower vine (*Pandorea jasminioides*) bought last summer. This bloomed spectacularly on the staging, producing many pink flowers with darker throats. It has come through winter well in my lightly heated office, where a minimum of 5°C (45°F) can be guaranteed.

I had intended to keep it in a pot, but I changed my mind and decided to wait until April. Then I'll plant it out in the greenhouse border, water and feed it well and let it grow up inside the roof. I'll have to lift and pot it in the autumn but I can't resist the temptation to let it run wild. For now, I'll train its wayward stems to a tripod of slim, home-grown bamboo canes and reduce some of the weaker stems by a third.

More to sow

Other jobs tackled recently include sowing hardy annuals, such as *Ammi majus*. I'll sow three or four seeds per module and eventually plant each one out as a small clump. Other bedding (like nicotiana) is generally sown into smallish pots, to be germinated in the propagating case and then transplanted to modules or pots.

Cuttings rooted towards the end of last summer were tackled too, including different kinds of pelargoniums. I'd like to build a collection of these again, as they are so good under glass and on the patio.

Step by step ➤ Potting up pelargoniums

ADD COMPOST
Rooted last autumn, this plant is being treated to its own 3½in (9cm) pot of 50:50 John Innes No2 and soilless potting compost.

WATER IN
After potting the young plants are watered in thoroughly, but gently, using a small can with a fine rose fitted to the end.

SETTING OUT
All three of these plants were rooted in one pot. The smallest is a bit weak, but increasing light and warmth will help it to catch up.

Your gardening week

Caring for seedlings

After seeds germinate, there's work to do before plants can go out in the garden...

FOLLOWING GOOD germination, a greenhouse, conservatory, windowsill or coldframe can quickly fill up with young plants. Having got your seeds to sprout, the hard work begins. Some seedlings may fail – that's survival of the fittest for you – but there is much you can do to ensure the majority grow into good, sturdy plants ready to be planted out. Check on, or tend to seedlings daily. Here are six tips to get them through:

Water wisely

■ Never allow seedlings to dry out totally. Check compost every day, even if you don't always give more water. And don't use rainwater for seedlings, as it contains many impurities and can encourage fungal diseases and rots (it is, of course, OK for woody and mature plants, but seedlings are too delicate).

Ventilation

■ As sunlight strengthens throughout spring, a greenhouse can get very hot very quickly. If seedlings are subjected to too high a temperature they may wilt, and this can sometimes cause permanent damage. So make sure that you ventilate the greenhouse (or coldframe) on clear days. If you work during the day, open vents or the door a chink, before you set off. And make sure you close it again at night.

Damping off

■ This is a fungal disease that can attack most kinds of seedlings. The little plantlets just collapse, seemingly for no reason. Even more baffling, some can be affected while others close to them remain perfectly OK. Copper-based Cheshunt Compound was the traditional preventative, but this is no longer available. Bayer Fruit & Vegetable Disease Control can be used as a suitable alternative.

Pricking out

■ Give your seedlings room to grow, by pricking them out and potting up individually. If you don't, they will compete for light and nutrients, becoming pale, elongated and malformed. Once they have their first set of true leaves use

a dibber or pencil to gently loosen them from the compost and, holding the leaves, transfer to their own pots or cells. Avoid damaging roots and stems, as this will almost certainly kill them. If leaves get bruised more will soon develop.

Potting up

■ When seedlings sown or pricked out into individual cells or modules have filled the space with roots, they can be potted up. Gently remove the whole plant, with its rootball intact, by pushing it out from the base. Place the plant centrally in a pot filled with John Innes No2 or multi-purpose compost, gently firm it in and water. From now on plants can endure slightly cooler conditions during the day.

A little protection

■ Nights can still be cold – and often frosty until June – so it does make sense to have some horticultural fleece handy to drape over the developing young plants by night. You could also use lightweight, bubble wrap or newspaper. Always remove the covering each morning. If the plants are very long or flimsy, it is not wise to allow the covering to rest on them, so support it above them using tall upturned pots or pea sticks as a frame.

Rays of Spring Sunshine

Martyn Cox takes a look at the much-loved daffodil, and offers his choice of the 10 best for different garden situations

Narcissus 'Pinza' is one of the sunniest-looking daffodils varieties

THERE ARE some 50 species of daffodils, and breeding work has led to the introduction of thousands of varieties, with more and more appearing each year. My advice is not to be overwhelmed by this seemingly infinite choice – simply buy daffodils that you like the look of and that will suit your garden.

If you have a courtyard, terrace or even a balcony, bulbs can be grown in pots. Rather than grow lots of different varieties together, keep things simple and grow a single variety in a container. Pick low growing varieties such as 'Jack Snipe', 'Tête-à-Tête' and 'Thalia'

Daffodils are essential in garden beds and borders. Avoid growing them in regimented rows like bedding plants, aiming instead for informal drifts or large clumps. Dot them among perennials that will fill the gaps left after they die back later in the season.

They are perfect with herbaceous peonies, but their colour associates well with blue, so you could team them up with pulmonarias or other spring bulbs, such as the grape hyacinth (*Muscari latifolium*).

One thing you could try at planting time this autumn is what I refer to as 'lasagne-like' planting. It is so-called because you plant three different varieties of bulbs – in layers – in a large pot or tub, somewhat like the famous dish.

Between late August and late November, put a layer of compost into the bottom of a 12in (30cm) container and into this you plant some tulip bulbs. Cover these with 2in (5cm) of compost, and then

If you only have a small balcony or patio, grow low varieties such as Narcissus cyclamineus (pictured), 'Jack Snipe' and 'Tête-à-Tête'

Try the 'lasagne' method, planting during autumn in pots in layers with bulbs such as iris and tulips

BEST FOR POTS:
'Tête-à-Tête' – golden yellow flowers appear during February and March. H 6in (15cm).

BEST FOR UNUSUAL FLOWERS:
'Cum Laude' – hibiscus-like flowers with white perianth and pink cups. H 14in (35cm).

BEST FOR EARLY FLOWERS:
'Cedric Morris' – slightly ragged yellow trumpets appear as early as December and last into February. H 10in (25cm).

BEST FOR LATE FLOWERS:
Narcissus poeticus var. *recurvus* – known as the pheasant's eye narcissus. White perianth with yellow trumpet edged with red; appearing in May. H 16in (40cm).

BEST FOR NATURALISING:
'February Gold' – uniform golden yellow flowers with slightly nodding heads during February and March. H 12in (30cm).

BEST IN BEDS:
'Cheerfulness' – multi-headed variety with creamy white, scented blooms in mid-spring. H 15in (38cm).

BEST WHITE FLOWERS:
'Thalia' – this cultivar produces up to four graceful white flowers per stalk. Good for pots. H 10in (25cm).

BEST DOUBLE FLOWERS:
'Rip Van Winkle' – golden yellow flowers appear during March and April. The perianth is divided into a mass of narrow segments, giving it a slightly ragged look. H 5in (13cm).

BEST FOR ROCK GARDENS:
Narcissus bulbocodium subsp. *obesus* 'Diamond Ring' – a tiny plant with several yellow trumpets on each stem. H 4in (10cm).

BEST FOR SCENT:
'Golden Dawn' – heavily perfumed flowers in April. Tangerine orange cup surrounded by yellow perianth. H 16in (40cm)

add daffodils. Cover as before and finish with a layer of dwarf irises. Top up with compost and water the whole lot in.

In late winter the display will begin with the small bulbous irises, followed by the daffodils, and end with the tulips in May.

Or, of course, you could plant the daffodils in the 'naturalised' way: those with simple flowers can look absolutely stunning when emerging through grass. This technique is equally attractive whether you've got a tiny emerald sward sitting at the back of a town garden or rolling acres of grassland.

Choose early-flowering varieties if possible, as you won't be able to mow the grass until the bulbs have completely died back after flowering, a process that can take up to six weeks.

GROWING ADVICE

Feeding:

■ Clumps that have been in the ground for more than a year will benefit from a feed. Water some tomato food around them twice whilst they're in flower. The potash in this feed will promote flowers next year.

Deadheading:

■ Save the plant from wasting energy, by regularly pinching off the faded flowers. Make sure you also remove the bulbous ovary behind the flower.

Weeding:

■ Be vigilant over weeds; remove any growing between the bulbs.

Dead foliage:

■ At the end of the flowering period, leave the plants alone until such time as the foliage has died and turned brown. With later-flowering types this could be as late as June or even July. Then remove the leaves to tidy the area. Either lift the bulbs and store them before replanting sound specimens from late August onwards, or you can leave them where they are in the soil.

Gardener's tea break

CROSSWORD...

just for fun Answers below

SPOT THE DIFFERENCE

Seeds and young plants need maximum light levels for strong growth in spring, so it's always worth giving the greenhouse a quick scrub. But can you spot the **FOUR** differences between these two pictures? (Answers can be found at the bottom of the page)

ACROSS

1 The poppy genus (7)
6 Name for a plant that produces two seed leaves (11)
7 One does this with turf (4)
8 The rose genus (4)
9 Not wet, as in the laundry – and husbandry! (3)
10 Pile or mass, as in compost! (4)
11 Large South American flightless bird, not a hare! (4) (anag)
13 Some herbs are grown and used in this way (11)
14 The force or energy of collisions of objects (7)

DOWN

1 It's like a petal, but you put your foot on it to move forward! (5)
2 Genus of evergreen creeping perennials, in the box family (11)
3 The dog's tooth violet genus (11)
4 Having an affinity for water; able to absorb, or be wetted by water (11)
5 Genus of the Indian shot plant (5)
10 Natural organic compounds in the soil, formed from the decomposition of plant and animal residues (5)
12 Bottomless or unfathomed depth (5)

Problem solver

Q June Monks asks: "The frog spawn in my pond has disintegrated. In the past we've had hundreds of tadpoles so what has gone wrong this time?"

A The cause is fish – sticklebacks or minnows – eating the eggs. Dragonfly larvae could be devouring it, too. Frogs may return and lay more spawn. If so, use a clean bucket to lift some water and the spawn from the pond. Place the bucket in a sheltered area and allow the tadpoles to grow.

THE SCENT OF SPRING

ON A recent mild, sunny day I walked through the garden and my nose caught the most heavenly, beautiful scent. I knew I didn't have any scented shrubs in the garden, but eventually tracked the wonderful smell down to a small clump of crocus, touched by sunlight. How marvellously uplifting – nature's hint to let us know spring isn't far off.
Stephen Gaulter, Malmesbury, Wilts

Bob is a panellist on BBC Gardeners' Question Time and an avid recycler

The Organic Gardener *Bob Flowerdew*

Sacrificial planting

Growing sacrificial or 'trapping' crops is good organic practice, says Bob

WE'RE GARDENERS. We grow plants. But pests are problems and, if left to do their worst, can destroy our hard work.

Sacrificial and trap plants are cheap solutions to many pest problems. They may not be complete solutions, but certainly they are effective in reducing pest populations.

I noticed in a trial of autumn-sown onions that the variety 'Buffalo' was crawling with slugs. These pests seemed to be ignoring other varieties. Rather than avoiding growing 'Buffalo', why not mix it with another variety. Then the slugs auto-thin the row for you!

Likewise, imagine a ring of freshly planted out Chinese cabbage around your hostas – do you think slugs will bother the latter while their preferred food survives so close nearby. The cabbage has become a sacrificial plant.

If, one evening, you lift away the cabbage plants with the slugs aboard, then they have become trap plants.

French beans growing under cover lure red spider from sweetcorn. Strawberries in my vine tubs give early warning of vine weevils – by dying first.

Sacrificial plants can be even more of the same – I grow lots of vines (of the variety 'Boskoop Glory'), yet the birds still get at my grapes. So I've planted more to run over a couple of (unpopular) apple trees. These vines produce prodigious crops, which fobs off the birds a while.

> *"The edges of massed plantings suffer most damage from pests"*

By the way, it is the edges of massed plantings that suffer most damage from mobile pests so, where possible, grow a bigger block simply to sustain the losses.

'Trap plants' are the neatest solutions – every pest has a favourite snack, and as we provide these we lure the pests onto them. Then we whisk them off together to the compost heap, or worse (for the pest!).

Sweet tobacco plants are a lure for whiteflies; broad beans for red spider mites. Grow either in pots, nestle these amongst the infestation and again dispose of a week later.

Spare potatoes going over and sprouting are very attractive to mealy-bug; place them in amongst infested plants, then remove and dispose of them a week later. It's simple and cheap.

Do it now → Topical advice Getting the best from your organic garden

Start the first session of lawnmowing with your blades set really high, then next time lower it a tad

Add a measure of seaweed feed to all your waterings now, to provide trace elements for your plants

Weeds are now germinating in profusion, so the organic motto is to hoe early – and to also hoe often!

Your gardening week

Ornamental garden

Planting summer bulbs

Spring is the time to plant bulbs that are at their most glorious during summer

SPRING-FLOWERING bulbs should still be in bloom, but it's worth thinking ahead to summer flowering bulbs and what they can offer later in the year. Mid-March, particularly in the south of the country, is a good time to plant out some of the hardier summer bulbs, tubers and corms.

While the more tender begonias and dahlias may have been in the coldframe for several weeks now, others can be put straight into beds and borders as the soil starts to warm up. Ideally wait until soil temperatures reach 13°C (55°F) or above to reduce the risk of bulbs rotting.

Summer bulbs are ideal for growing in pots, planting in clumps (for impact) and dotting about in your border to add colour or fill gaps. Most will do well in a warm, sunny position in free-draining soil.

Free-draining soil is a must; summer bulbs are more susceptible to rotting in damp conditions than spring bulbs. If you have heavy, clay soil, you'll need to dig in lots of coarse sand or grit – a full bucket to each square metre. If your garden is shaded, it's best to hold off planting until late April or to start your bulbs off earlier in pots in a warmer, brighter location.

There are so many different types of summer bulbs and most garden centres stock a good range through spring. Pick the packets that are dry, fresh, mould-free and have the biggest bulbs in them.

Pot up spare bulbs

■ IF YOU'RE planning to use your bulbs in beds and borders, it's worth planting several different varieties in pots, particularly if you have bulbs you can't fit in your border space. Later in the season these can be slotted into any gaps that may appear as other plants finish or fail to perform how you expected.

Step by step ▶ Planting summer bulbs in the border

1 Planting hole depth needs to be two to three times the bulb's length. For smaller bulbs, like these acidanthera, it is easier to dig one big hole and add compost and grit to the bottom.

2 Place the bulbs into the hole with the growing point upwards. Don't squeeze bulbs in – space them 2in (5cm) apart, and if they don't fit, widen the hole and try again, or put fewer of them in.

3 Cover them with soil and gently firm it down. Place a cane with a plant label attached over the planted area so they are not accidently dug up later in the season.

Top bulbs to try

- Crocosmia
- Agapanthus
- Anemone de Caen (pic)
- Acidanthera
- Tigridia
- Alliums
- Freesia

Five jobs for top summer bulb displays

■ Once your bulbs put up leaves and stems, these five tasks will ensure the plants stay healthy and put on a great summer show

1 Pot up spare bulbs

■ POT-GROWN bulbs should go outside now. These liatris plants were potted up as dry bulbs in April and are being planted out in early June. Similar treatment may be given to any summer bulbs. Bulbs potted up and grown under cover will produce earlier blooms compared to bulbs planted directly out in late April or May. If you don't get around to potting any, garden centres offer a range of potted, pre-sprouted bulbs for summer planting.

2 Staking and tying

■ TALLER GROWING bulbs including gladioli, dahlias and lilies, need supporting. Gladioli can be grown in rows for cut flower plants; and here they need to be attached to a framework of wires supported by stout posts. In the garden it is more pleasing to the eye if they are individually staked with bamboo canes. Large pea sticks (dark green) make a more subtle addition to the display when used instead of bamboo supports. Ensure ties do not choke developing stems.

3 Feeding

■ BULBS YOU intend to leave in the ground for future years should be fed after flowering. This enables them to build up reserves for next year. Between the end of flowering and foliage die-back, feed plants twice with granular or liquid feeds. Dahlias are particularly heavy feeders and appreciate a high potash liquid tomato feed when in flower, and afterwards.

4 Watering

■ BULBS CAN suffer if kept too dry, particularly those in pots. Watering should ideally be done by hand with a watering can. Avoid wetting foliage, as wet leaves can scorch in hot sun. If you must water overhead, do this late in the afternoon or evening. Alternatively, set out a seep hose or drip system for efficient soil watering.

5 Disbudding dahlias

■ TO GET bigger blooms on dahlias, remove most of the flower buds as they grow. This means removing all buds developing in leaf axils, leaving the bud at the stem tip to flower. All energy goes to this flower, which gets bigger as a result. Also remove low side shoots, to encourage longer stems.

Your gardening week

How to grow
Carrots

Sweet, crunchy and colourful roots

Varieties to try
'Amsterdam Forcing' – Very early, long, sweet stems

'Flyaway' – Tasty roots, resistant to carrot fly

'Autumn King' – Large rooted maincrop, stands well

SIMPLE STEPS

SITE & SOIL
■ CHOOSE A sunny, sheltered spot with deep, free-draining but moisture-retentive soil. Remove stones if possible. Carrots do best in a bed manured for a previous crop, as fresh manure can make roots fork. Rake in balanced fertiliser (2oz per sq yd) before sowing.

WHEN TO SOW
■ SOW EARLY varieties from February to June under cloches. Sow maincrop varieties from April to early August.

HOW TO SOW
■ PICK OUT larger stones and rake soil to a fine tilth. Draw straight drills, ½in (1cm) deep and 6in/15cm (early) to 8in/20cm (maincrop) apart. Water the drills thoroughly, then sow freshly bought seeds very thinly, spacing seeds ¼in (6mm) apart (pic 1). Cover with a very

fine sprinkling of old potting compost, mark the rows and cover with fleece or very fine meshed plastic

ROUTINE CARE
■ SEEDLINGS EMERGE in 2-3 weeks. Protect from slugs and snails. When big enough to handle, thin to 1in (2.5cm) apart (pic 2). Water regularly in dry spells. Thin again 4-5 weeks later to 2in (5cm) apart; for maincrop types thin once more to 3-4in (7.5-10cm) apart. Cover crops from late May with fleece to beat carrot fly

HARVEST
■ CHECK ROOTS by scraping back a little soil around the neck of the plant. Pull mature roots from the soil (pic 3) using a trowel to lift if necessary. Water to settle remaining roots after lifting some. Lift

and store maincrops in late autumn.

GROW IN POTS
■ SOW SEEDS very thinly over the surface of good, moist multipurpose or potting compost in deep, wide pots (min 8in x 8in/20cm x 20cm). Cover with a very fine sprinkling of compost. Care for as above.

Smartideas

Carrots will stand for several weeks in the soil, but it's best to sow a short row every two weeks through spring and summer, choosing early and maincrop varieties, to ensure a steady supply of fresh roots. In winter they can be lifted, foliage twisted off and stored buried in just-moist sand or peat.

Quick tips

March
...more things to do

1 Spring rolls!

■ SAVE MONEY and space by using toilet or kitchen roll tubes for seed sowing. These are great for long-rooted veg such as runner beans. Once grown big enough for outdoor planting they can be put straight into the soil, as the cardboard will decompose.

2 Covers on

■ LATE FROSTS can ruin cropping potential on early-flowering cherries, apricots, nectarines and peaches. Over night, cover dwarf trees or wall-trained fans and espaliers with horticultural fleece. Remove in the morning to allow pollinating insects to do their job.

3 Covers off

■ START TO remove cloches and soft coverings from vegetable crops during the day so plants can make the most of the day light. Re-cover each evening – especially if frosts are forecast.

4 Prune cornus

■ IF YOU want vibrant winter stems on your cornus (dogwood) plants next year, prune now before 'bud break' to encourage colourful, whippy growth. Pruned like this the shrubs will not flower in summer, but will look stunning on a dull winter's day. Cut back hard to just a few inches above the ground.

5 Protect raised beds

■ WOODEN RAISED beds need annual maintenance to prevent deterioration of the wood. Use linseed oil as a protective barrier. Apply on a dry, sunny day. Raw linseed oil can take several days to dry. Boiled linseed oil should dry within a day.

7 Top dress containers

■ PERMANENT CONTAINER displays will benefit from a bit of attention this month. Remove any weed growth and scrape off the top couple of inches of compost. Apply a sprinkling of fish, blood and bone then top up with fresh compost.

6 Tubers for cuttings

■ START DAHLIA, chrysanthemum and begonia tubers into growth now indoors. Some early growth can then be removed and used as cuttings to create more plants that will still flower this season. Once frosts have finished the 'parent' tubers can be planted out in the garden for late season flowering.

APRIL 2013

MONDAY

1

TUESDAY

2

WEDNESDAY

3

THURSDAY

4

FRIDAY

5

SATURDAY

6

SUNDAY

7

MONDAY

8

Spring pond care

I F YOU own a pond, there are plenty of jobs you should be getting on with during April.

New aquatic plants
■ This is the best time of year to introduce new aquatic plants to your pond. Bunches of weighted oxygenating plants are just dropped directly into the water, but containerised aquatics should be placed carefully into the water. Support the plant on bricks so that its young shoots just reach the surface. Remove the bricks, one by one, as the plant grows.

Divide waterlilies
■ A waterlily in need of dividing will have crowded leaves thrusting upwards, not lying flat. Lift the plant; ease it out of its basket and rinse off the soil. Remove open leaves, and cut the rhizome into two or more pieces, each having vigorous young roots. Plant each divided part in a pot using aquatic compost, with its crown just below soil level, and top with gravel.

Clear algae
■ Blanket weed is a form of algae resembling wet, green cotton wool. If left to grow it will choke the pond. Twirl stick or rake around in the water and gather it up like spaghetti on a fork. To prevent build-up, pond filters with UV lights can be installed; or sink a ball of barley straw in netting into the water.

Feed fish
■ As temperatures rise fish become more active. Fat reserves that sustained them during winter will now be used up. To restore their energy and improve health generally before the breeding season, scatter a few food pellets or flakes on the water surface.

APRIL 2013

TUESDAY

9

WEDNESDAY

10

THURSDAY

11

FRIDAY

12

SATURDAY

13

SUNDAY

14

MONDAY

15

TUESDAY

16

Supporting tall plants

YOU CAN get ahead with staking tall and climbing flowering plants – and crops like runner beans – which will grow tall later in the season by making plant supports, such as obelisks. Bamboo canes and twine are strong, cheap and easy to get hold of.

Putting them in place now will save time later, and with flowering perennials, will also look more natural as the plant smothers the support and hides it from view.

How to make an obelisk

Ideal for supporting peas, beans and other seasonal climbers, make an obelisk by placing a circle of five or six canes around your plant, or on the intended growing site, and tie together at the top to form a pyramid shape. Then every 10in (25cm) down the pyramid, wrap pieces of twine around the circumference of the structure and tie them in place, to provide more purchase for your climbing plants.

Other can arrangements, such as tripods, or squares of with pea netting, can be used depending on the plants' requirements. Or use twiggy 'pea sticks' (winter prunings from shrubs), pushed into the soil around the plants.

APRIL 2013

WEDNESDAY

17

THURSDAY

18

FRIDAY   RHS SHOW CARDIFF

19

SATURDAY   RHS SHOW CARDIFF

20

SUNDAY   RHS SHOW CARDIFF

21

MONDAY

22

TUESDAY

23

WEDNESDAY

24

Time to tidy pot plants

POT-GROWN plants, such as bay trees, olives, box balls and other long-term potted ornamentals will be shrugging off the winter now, and need a little TLC to perform well in the year ahead.

Trim off dead foliage and stems, and inspect leaves for signs of pests such as scale insects, (if you find any, deal with them using appropriate chemical or organic controls). Next, scrape off the top 1-2in (2.5-5cm) of compost around the plant, carefully, with a trowel or hand fork, and replace it with fresh John Innes No 3 compost. Check that the drainage hole in the base of the container is not blocked, and remove any slugs nestling there, or around the base and rim of the container.

Then give the container a liquid general feed, and position it in a sheltered spot in good light to stimulate new growth.

Finally, set the container on pot feet – which permits good drainage, and keeps ants out!

APRIL 2013

THURSDAY

25

FRIDAY

26

SATURDAY

27

SUNDAY

28

MONDAY

29

TUESDAY

30

Feeding plants in the borders

ESTABLISHED BORDERS packed with shrubs and perennials are often given little attention other than annual pruning, dividing congested plants, or squeezing in one or two extra. But those stalwarts of the garden will eventually use up the nutrients in the soil around their roots, and start to look tired and flower poorly.

Feeding every year in spring will give them a real boost and ensure they continue to flourish for years to come. Balanced fertilisers such as pelleted chicken manure, or granular Growmore, should be scattered around the root area of shrubs, and between perennials. Measuring is difficult, but 2-3 handfuls around a vigorous shrub will do the trick.

If the soil is dry, water the fertiliser in thoroughly. Mulch the area with a couple of inches depth of garden compost, composted bark or similar. The mulch will hold moisture in the soil and eventually break down to improve soil structure.

You could also feed the borders again in mid-autumn – but only with bonemeal to promote root growth. Balanced fertilisers can cause harm if used late in the season.

Your gardening week

Ornamental garden

Plant up a hanging basket

If you have a greenhouse, late April to May is a great time to get hanging baskets established

THERE'S STILL cold weather during this period, so if you haven't got a frost-free greenhouse or conservatory, leave planting your basket until mid-May. If you have, planting it in late April will give plants a chance to settle in and be raring to grow once set outside in late May.

There are lots of different basket styles available – wire types to use with a felt lining, wire types with moss lining, and wicker baskets – both rounded and pointed at the base, with built-in plastic lining. Garden centres and DIY stores will be bursting at the seams with bedding plants over the next few weeks, and deciding what to fill your baskets with is a problem to relish! A well planted and cared for basket should provide colour well into autumn. Read on for planting and care tips.

Which lining material?

■ FELT LININGS seem to have overtaken the traditional sphagnum moss lining in recent years. This stems from a perception that moss is not sourced in a sustainable way and so is not environmentally friendly.

Companies do however harvest sphagnum moss in a responsible way and the process has little damaging effect on the bog environments it is taken from. I use moss when I can find it at the garden centre, as moss looks better, and I don't like the smell of felt linings – but they work well enough.

Step by step

Planting a 12in (30cm) petunia basket with fuchsia centre and lobelia side planting

1 Line your basket and half fill with compost. Add slow release fertiliser and water retaining granules and mix well. If there are no planting holes, cut slits for side plants (in this case lobelia).

2 Insert side plants, roots first, from the outside of the basket. Wrapping rootballs in strips of plastic will make them easier to push through the planting holes, with less risk of damaging the plants.

3 Cover the exposed rootballs with compost then put in the top plants (aim to have their rootballs 1in/2.5cm below basket rim). Place the fuchsia in the centre and arrange 5-6 petunias around it.

4 Fill gaps around the roots with compost and tap the basket to settle in. Water well. Hang in a warm, bright spot in the greenhouse or conservatory. Harden off in late May to hang outside.

1 Hardening-off

■ IF YOU have planted your baskets early they will need hardening-off before going outside permanently. Starting in late May (depending on the weather!) place them outside during the day and bring back under cover at night. Do this for up to two weeks. But watch out for frosts, even hardened-off plants can be killed by a heavy late frost.

2 Hanging and siting

■ DON'T POSITION your hanging basket in an out-of-the-way spot – make sure it can be seen! You'll need to install hanging brackets, but before drilling holes and screwing in place, make sure the bracket extends out far enough for your chosen basket size to hang freely.

3 Compost

■ MOST MULTIPURPOSE composts will do for a hanging basket, but there are several specialist tub and basket composts available such as the pictured Miracle Gro moisture control compost. These composts contain wetting agents – if you're using them don't add more water retaining granules! They also have a high level of fertiliser to promote strong growth and bigger flowers.

4 Feeding and watering

■ WITH SO many plants crammed into a basket, they won't make it through the season without extra feeding. Add slow release granular fertiliser to the compost when planting. After six to eight weeks apply a liquid feed every two weeks or so to get them through to autumn.

The compost in a hanging basket dries out very quickly – add water retaining gel when planting the basket – one teaspoon of granules should be enough for a 12in (30cm) basket. Water daily, morning or evening, even both in very hot weather, until water drips from the bottom of the basket.

Ongoing care

Once in flower deadhead regularly for repeat flowering through the season. Check compost regularly for dryness – water as needed to avoid drying out. Gaps may appear – replace individual spent plants as needed to maintain the display. Liquid feed every two weeks – more often if plants become sluggish or start to turn yellow. Add more compost if it has settled in the basket or washed out of the lining.

Your gardening week

Ornamental garden

How to grow sweet peas

Cheerful colour and sensational fragrance make sweet peas an essential ingredient of the summer garden

SNIFFING THE first fragrant sweet peas of the year is one of gardening's greatest pleasures. Growers of sweet peas (*Lathyrus odoratus*) tend to fall into one of two camps. Most buy their seed around now, and get them growing for flowering in three or four months' time.

Then there are those who are deadly serious about their plants. They sow in autumn, and overwinter the young plants to encourage them to flower a month or so earlier than the spring-sown types.

Both approaches are absolutely fine. But if you're a first-time grower, or you're time-pressed, or have no facility to overwinter plants, now is a good time to sow. There are hundreds of different varieties available from a host of different suppliers. But check that the packet says the flowers you've chosen are scented – some hybrids are not.

Neither should you be seduced by the perennial sweet pea (*Lathyrus latifolius*) which is amazingly vigorous and floriferous, but has no scent.

Buy annual varieties, check the packet says they're scented, and you'll enjoy all the benefits of exquisite sweet pea flowers.

Seeds can be sown in a variety of ways – in small pots, four or five seeds to a pot to be teased apart for planting out later; in tall containers, singly as we've demonstrated here, or directly in the soil where they are to grow. Starting seeds in containers under cover will get them growing quicker, so you'll have flowers earlier.

Why not sow both indoors and outside to give a succession of flowers through the summer?

Sweet peas need support to about 6ft (1.8m). A simple wigwam of canes wrapped around with string will do, or use pea netting strung between canes, or a shop-bought obelisk for a smarter finish.

The soil should be deep and rich – improved with garden compost, well-rotted manure or similar – and the site should be sheltered from strong winds, and be sunny.

Step by step Sowing sweet peas under cover

Collect toilet roll centres – they make ideal deep containers for sowing sweet peas, and can be planted directly into the soil

1 Soaking your sweet pea seeds in water overnight can help to prime them for germination

2 Fill toilet roll centres with a good multipurpose compost and stand them in a plastic container

3 Press one of the soaked seeds into the compost, ½in (1cm) deep, and cover with a compost

4 Water well, then stand them on a sunny windowsill, or in a heated propagator at 20-25°C (68-77°F)

5 In 7 – 21 days seeds will appear. Ventilate well, keep moist, and when roots show harden plants off

---

3 steps to bigger sweet peas

■ GET BIGGER flowers from this garden favourite with three simple tricks:

1 ■ Two weeks after planting out, choose the strongest stem on each plant and tie it to a support using twine or a wire/plastic ring. Remove all other shoots, and continue to do so as the main shoot grows.

2 ■ Remove all tendrils and sideshoots except the one immediately below the growing tip, just in case the leader is damaged by birds or bad weather. Do this regularly. Tie the main stem to its support with string as it grows.

3 ■ Remove early flowers to conserve energy for larger blooms later in the year. Soil should be well prepared ahead of planting, but for an added boost, liquid feed plants as the main crop of buds starts to develop.

Planting pot- raised sweet pea seedlings

■ Water the seedlings and allow to drain before planting out in the soil or in a container.

■ Use multipurpose compost in containers, enriched with garden compost or well rotted horse manuure.

■ In small containers add slow release fertiliser and water retaining granules.

■ In open ground add well rotted manure to the soil where you plan to plant.

The formal area closest to the Blays' house is framed by a clipped Lonicera nitida 'Baggesen's Gold' hedge planted in a wavy serpentine shape. It provides a gentle border between the formal garden and wild area beyond. The steep sides of the chine are joined by a traditional wooden bridge.

Our valley view

Words by Sue Bradley / **Photography** Peter Chatterton

John and **Jeannie Blay** embarked on a steep learning curve when they took on their chine garden on the Dorset coast

Garden notes

Name: John and Jeannie Blay

Address: Poole, Dorset

Size of garden: Half-an-acre

Soil type: Sandy and slightly acidic

Special features: This seven year old garden stands in a Dorset chine (small valley) lined with Purbeck Stone. A formal area near the house has lawn, sub-tropical species, clipped hedging and Palladian rotunda. This opens up to a wilder space filled with colourful shrubs and mature trees. Steep slopes lead to a small pond. The slightly damper climate in this area is ideal for ferns and lilies.

Season visited: Spring

THE GARDEN at Chine View overlooks a steep sided valley that plunges some 70 feet to the sea. This dramatic backdrop, from which John and Jeannie Blay's home takes its name, is matched by a flamboyant collection of plants that stand out like glistening jewels against moss-covered Purbeck stone.

Things were somewhat different seven years ago, however, when the Blays moved into the new build. The garden, laid out in the 1980's, had been ravaged for more than a decade by brambles, ivy and other invasive weeds, then trampled by builders' boots.

But, undeterred, like modern day Prince Charmings, the Blays' slashed through the thorns to reveal their sleeping beauty and bring her back to life.

The transformation is all the more remarkable given that John and Jeannie had come to gardening relatively late in life. The couple had just retired from demanding professional careers in the Midlands. Not the kind of people to shrink from a challenge, however, they armed themselves with the knowledge and skills they would need before setting about transforming Chine View. Jeannie went on a two-year RHS course which included work experience in the gardens at Compton Acres, close to her home. "It's got the same steep banks as we have here and some visitors call our garden a corner of Compton Acres," says Jeannie. Once the mammoth job of clearing their canvas had been completed, John and Jeannie turned their attention to filling it with colour and interest.

> **66 It's got the same steep banks as we have here and some visitors call our garden a corner of Compton Acres 99**

Chine View draws a variety of wildlife, including squirrels, foxes and woodpeckers. Here a bird feeder provides a ready store of peanuts for a cheeky mouse which managed to squeeze inside!

The drop away from the house is quite spectacular. A variety of shrubs to add texture and colour to their garden – fuchsias add dainty detail in contrast to vibrant blooms from rhododendrons and azaleas.

John's favourite rhododendron is 'Sappho' with its purple eye and white surround.

John and Jeannie's creative pieces include birds and animals made from recycled chicken wire and barbed wire. Amongst them are geese (pictured) foxes and a bustard.

Fortunately some of the garden's original features remained, and the couple used the existing mature trees and sculptural conifers, along with a Palladian rotunda and a serpentine hedge, as their starting point.

By chance, the Blays' met the elderly woman under whose direction the garden was planned. "We learned that 330 tonnes of Purbeck stone from Swanage was used when the entire garden was originally laid out," says John.

> ❝ We learned that 330 tonnes of Purbeck stone from Swanage was used when the entire garden was originally laid out ❞

"It took two men six months to move the stone in 1979, and they did an excellent job.

However, today's garden at Chine View is very much the couple's own masterpiece and reflects their creative and engaging personalities. "We've used the hedge and the rotunda to create a more formal feel closest to our home, before it opens into a wilder environment beyond", John explains.

"It's not a normal garden and sometimes we feel like a pair of mountain goats!" adds Jeannie.

SUB-TROPICAL TYPES

The Blays' have filled the area closest to the house with striking sub-tropical plant species such as phormium, *Trachycarpus fortunei* (Chusan palm) and *Yucca aloifolia*, which all thrive in Dorset's warmer climate. Most of them need very little maintenance, with only one variety requiring the protection of horticultural fleece when the temperature drops.

While the Blays' have purchased many unusual plants, they have also developed a keen eye for bargains. "Our yuccas were tiny when we bought them at a charity sale," explains John. "Friends who live locally also give us plants that they have split from ones growing in their gardens.

"We also bring on a few of our own garden plants from cuttings, and I've been trying to grow cordyline from seed. We like to experiment and learn."

Rhododendrons thrive in the sandy and slightly acidic soil found in Poole. "We've noticed that they come out in colour order," says John. "They start with white, going on to pinks, reds and purples."

Your gardening week

Ornamental garden

Plant summer containers

The popular summer bedding plants aren't just for the garden borders

ANY OF the summer bedding varieties now on sale in garden centres can be placed in containers to brighten up patios, be they hanging baskets, terracotta, plastic, wood or metal pots. When grown on in containers these plants will need more attention than those planted out in beds and borders. In the heat of summer, pots will need daily watering, sometimes twice in particularly hot spells .

These vigorous plants will quickly use up the food in their compost so will need regular supplements though the season with a liquid feed containing all major nutrients. At the potting up stage it's worth adding some slow release fertiliser to the compost, but after six to eight weeks a fortnightly liquid feed will be necessary to keep plants flowering strongly. Stop feeding in late August.

When growing bedding in pots, use either a compost with added wetting agents, or add 'water retaining granules' to the mix, as well as a decorative mulch to help retain moisture.

Some bedding plants, such as the New Guinea impatiens will actually bloom better in pot-bound conditions. Most, including petunias, pelargoniums,

verbena and lobelia, are sun lovers too, making them great for hot spots in the garden – but that also means they won't perform particularly well in a shady position. If you're planning to site a pot in a shady spot, choose your plants carefully – foliage plants such as coleus and hostas do better in shade than flowering plants.

Fuchsias are a summer-flowering favourite and while there are small bedding plants sold by the thousand, why not try something different and go for a standard to bring height to the display. We're using a 12in (30cm) 'mini standard' (above right), underplanted with New Guinea impatiens. Follow the steps to get the look on your patio.

Instant colour fix

■ THESE VIBRANT SENETTI (*Pericallis x hybrida*) are sold in full bloom, making them a great choice for when instant colour is needed. After their first flush, cut plants back to 4in (10cm) and you'll get a second floral display later in the season. They're best kept in pots – if summer weather turns cold they won't perform well planted out in cool soils.

Step by step Plant a fuchsia feature pot

1 Fill your container with compost, slow release fertiliser and water retaining gel, so that the fuchsia rootball sits an inch below the pot rim. Add compost around the roots to raise the planting level

2 Insert the New Guinea impatiens around the fuchsia rootball – we managed to squeeze in six plants – and infill any gaps with compost so that no roots are left exposed. Gently firm in around plants

3 Water the pot well and allow to drain. If hollows appear in the compost, top up with more. Terracotta pots dry out quickly in summer sun so add a mulch of gravel or stone to help trap moisture

Plant a herb basket

■ CONTAINERS ARE a great place to grow all sorts of crops, as well as flowering plants. But some of the easiest and most rewarding edibles are herbs. A selection of woody herbs in a large terracotta pot such as sage, rosemary and thyme, can last for years if well looked after, providing flavourings for the kitchen, and flowers in season for you and the bees to enjoy.

Here we've taken a slightly different approach and planted up a wire shopping basket using the hanging basket technique of lining the container with moss. It looks great and should provide a steady supply of tasty leaves for the kitchen throughout summer with regular watering and occasional feeding.

Step by step PLANTS YOU'LL NEED:
Rosemary, oregano, mint, sage, thyme, chives

1 Line basket bottom with plastic (from a compost bag). Build up the sides with several layers of sphagnum moss. Part fill with multipurpose compost.

2 Site plants; pack compost around the rootballs. If the display will be viewed from one side only, remember to place larger plants at the back of the display.

3 Tease out dense rootballs before setting them in the basket (or container). Finalise planting, and infill around the rootballs with more compost.

4 Water in to settle the plants in the compost; add more compost if hollows appear. Feed plants twice a month after six to eight weeks.

Your gardening week

How to grow beetroot

Rob Keenan's small town garden proved ideal for raising a good crop of tasty beets

IN THE past couple of years I've added beetroot to my list of 'cooking' veg. My small town garden has room to grow only a handful of beetroot, but that's fine for me. I don't need too many of them.

If you do end up growing more than you need immediately, the roots store very well and, once cooked, can be pickled in vinegar.

Although you can buy individual 'monogerm' seeds, most packets contain little corky clusters of seeds – these should be left intact rather than split apart. As for beetroot's soil requirements, you're better off with a free-draining, sandy loam, but any reasonable quality soil will suffice. Just make sure the pH value isn't much below 6 (add lime if necessary) and remove as many stones as you can. Ideally, the bed should also get a good few hours of direct sunlight each day.

Prepare the soil by digging in garden compost or a small amount of well-rotted manure – but not too much as it can cause the roots to 'fork', (which also applies to other rootcrops, such as carrots.

Seeds can be sown outdoors in the soil from March (under cloches) until July. Sowing a few seeds every few weeks will mean you get roots maturing regularly throughout the summer and early autumn.

Seeds should germinate within a couple of weeks. Make sure the soil never dries out, and thin seedlings to one every 4in (10cm) as soon as they're big enough to handle.

Early sowings are particularly prone to bolting, so choose a bolt-resistant variety, such as 'Boltardy'.

Step by step
Follow Rob's easy guide for a great crop of beetroot next summer

1 Dig over the bed in the autumn or winter, removing stones and adding plenty of compost. If your soil is acidic add lime to bring the pH value to around 6.5-7.0

2 Lightly apply Growmore to the bed around a month before sowing. This will give the beetroot all the nutrients they'll need for the season ahead.

3 Sow in drills 1in (2.5cm) deep and 1ft (30cm) apart. Seeds should be spaced 4in (10cm) apart. Draw soil over seeds and water well.

4 Thin seedlings to the strongest one every 4in (10cm). Roots mature quickly. Don't let the roots grow larger than a cricket ball, as they can get woody.

Varieties to try

Feeling more adventurous? Try **'Alto'**, a purple fleshed cylindrical variety, or pretty purple and white ringed **'Chioggia Pink'**; or yellow **'Burpees Gold'**.

From left to right: 'Alto', 'Chioggia Pink', 'Burpees Gold'

April
...more things to do

① In the greenhouse

■ AT THIS time of year greenhouses are packed full of seedlings and young plants. Avoid confusion or planting the wrong plants in the wrong place in the garden by checking that all pots and trays are clearly labelled.

② Softwood cuttings

■ APRIL IS the start of the softwood cutting season. Take young shoots from the likes of hydrangea, buddleja, forsythia, fuchsia and magnolia, strip lower leaves and plant them in moist cuttings compost. Set trays or pots of cuttings in a covered propagator indoors, or cover with a clear plastic bag.

③ Pinch out chillies and peppers

■ CHILLIES AND peppers sown in January in the greenhouse can be pinched out as they reach around 6in (15cm) tall. This will encourage side branching, and bushy growth, leading to heavier crops through the season. Remove the growing tip to just above a leaf joint.

④ Watch out for nesting birds

■ TREES, SHRUBS and hedging may need some attention to keep them in shape, but before cutting into foliage check for signs of nesting birds. It is against the law to disturb nesting birds. If nests are seen, leave pruning until summer.

⑤ Mulch borders

■ MAKE THE most of April showers by trapping moisture in the soil. A 3in (7.5cm) layer of well rotted compost, manure, or bark chippings applied to the soil surface around plants will help retain water in the soil, and keep weeds down.

⑥ Citrus care

■ ORANGES, LEMONS and other citrus are hungry plants. Through winter they should have been placed indoors and given a winter feed (equal parts nitrogen, phosphate and potash). Plants can be moved outside now, but watch out for late frosts. Also, start to feed with a citrus-specific summer feed (high in nitrogen to boost growth and prevent fruit drop).

⑦ Divide daffodils

■ LIFT and divide congested daffodils to increase stocks while still in leaf, replanting straight away in other areas of the garden. Alternatively lift once foliage dies down, allow to dry out and store in a cool dry place for replanting in autumn.

MAY 2013

WEDNESDAY

1

THURSDAY

2

FRIDAY

3

SATURDAY

4

SUNDAY

5

MONDAY

6

TUESDAY

7

WEDNESDAY

8

Check soil acidity

ALL SOILS are acidic or alkaline to varying degrees, and this is measured on the pH scale. It affects what types of plant will thrive in your soil – for instance, azaleas won't do well in an alkaline soil in the shrub bed, while brassicas won't thrive on a veg plot soil that is acidic.

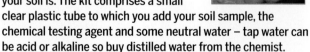

A simple kit can tell you what pH level your soil is. The kit comprises a small clear plastic tube to which you add your soil sample, the chemical testing agent and some neutral water – tap water can be acid or alkaline so buy distilled water from the chemist.

The soil sample should be taken from 2-3in (5-7cm) deep – let it dry out before testing. Shaken up then left to stand, the liquid in the tube will colour-up: compare this colour against a chart supplied with the kit.

The acidity of your garden soil should inform the type of plants you grow. Choose varieties that will thrive in your soil. Neutral soils (neither acidic nor alkaline) will support most types of plant. You can adjust acidic soil by adding garden lime, and make lime soils more acidic by adding sulphur chips – but these treatments need regular application.

MAY 2013

THURSDAY	RHS SPRING SHOW MALVERN
9	
FRIDAY	RHS SPRING SHOW MALVERN
10	
SATURDAY	RHS SPRING SHOW MALVERN
11	
SUNDAY	
12	
MONDAY	
13	
TUESDAY	
14	
WEDNESDAY	
15	
THURSDAY	
16	

Revitalise wooden garden furniture

RESTORING FADED and algae-covered wooden garden furniture is hard work, but it's cheaper than replacing it. The treatment will preserve the wood for years, and it'll look great when you've finished!

Step by step

Treating wood

1 Apply a treatment to remove algae and grime. We've used Clearway (🖱 www.clearwaybyotech.co.uk) as it safely works without the need for follow up jet spraying or scrubbing. The formula is diluted 1:9 with water and sprayed onto wood to kill and remove algae and mould.

Sand

2 Now sand off the dead algae. This is one of those jobs that seems to take forever, but it is worth it. To see fresh wood revealed is very satisfying. Use a power sander to speed things up, but you will need to get into nooks and crannies with a folded sand sheet. Use 100 or 120-grit sheets.

Stain

3 Remove sanding dust by wiping down all surfaces with white spirit before applying stains or paints. Stains not supplied with an applicator are best applied with a rag. Be sparing when loading the rag to avoid streaks – starting at the bottom and working up will also help avoid this.

MAY 2013

FRIDAY

17

GARDEN FESTIVAL, HILLSBOROUGH CASTLE, CO. DOWN, NORTHERN IRELAND

SATURDAY

18

GARDEN FESTIVAL, HILLSBOROUGH CASTLE, CO. DOWN, NORTHERN IRELAND

SUNDAY

19

GARDEN FESTIVAL, HILLSBOROUGH CASTLE, CO. DOWN, NORTHERN IRELAND

MONDAY

20

TUESDAY

21

RHS CHELSEA FLOWER SHOW

WEDNESDAY

22

RHS CHELSEA FLOWER SHOW

THURSDAY

23

RHS CHELSEA FLOWER SHOW

FRIDAY

24

RHS CHELSEA FLOWER SHOW

Enjoy the blossom!

MAY IS a marvellous time in the garden. In the borders, late spring flowering plants are still showing good colour while early summer blooms are just beginning to open. There could still be some daffodils and chaenomeles, the bigger irises are coming into their own, and roses are showing their first flowers alongside granny's bonnets, early hardy geraniums and *Clematis montana*.

But it's the trees and large shrubs that really excel at this time. Rhododendrons, azaleas, lilacs and apple trees are in full bloom, but the most glorious are the ornamental cherries in ice-cream mounds of pink and white.

Branches bend under the weight of large pink, double flowered forms such as 'Cheal's Weeping', shimmering whites like the wild cherry *Prunus avium*, and deliciously feminine pale pink blossoms like *P.* 'Hokusai' with flowers each 2in (5cm) across. One of the best garden forms is *Prunus incisa* 'Kojo-no-mai' (pictured above, a dwarfing tree growing to just 8ft (2.5m) tall. Like many cherries, the leaves on this form give good autumn colour, too.

MAY 2013

SATURDAY
RHS CHELSEA FLOWER SHOW

25

SUNDAY

26

MONDAY

27

TUESDAY

28

WEDNESDAY

29

THURSDAY
BLOOM 2013, DUBLIN

30

FRIDAY
GARDENING SCOTLAND, EDINBURGH

& BLOOM 2013, DUBLIN

31

TV gardener and designer Chris Beardshaw on his gold medal winning Furzey Gardens garden at the 2012 Chelsea Flower Show

RHS Chelsea Flower Show

IT'S THE pinnacle of gardening aspiration, gathering of the great and the good in horticulture, showing and sharing their expertise in growing and using plants. The Chelsea Flower Show, organised by The Royal Horticultural Society, is held at the end of May every year in the grounds of the Royal Hospital, Chelsea, in London. It is a fabulous opportunity to learn about new trends in gardening, see the very latest new plants launched onto the world stage, and be inspired by breathtaking (and occasionally outrageous) show garden designs.

The Great Pavilion, a massive covered area, houses displays by hundreds of the UK's leading specialist plant nurseries – plants are preened to perfection as the nurseries vie for coveted gold, silver or bronze medals.

Outdoors magnificent, manicured and sometimes outlandish show gardens, also battling for medal honours, offer the chance to explore new ideas and suggest new styles of design the ordinary gardener can copy. Be quick when tickets go on sale in the spring, as they always sell out! Visit ✌ **www. rhs.org.uk** for more information.

Ornamental garden

Your gardening week

Plant summer borders

Follow our advice on setting bedding plants out to fill your summer garden with colour

AS THE WEATHER WARMS, with night temperatures often above 10°C (50°F), those of us who have been patiently growing tender bedding plants in our greenhouses, or resisting them in garden centre aisles, can now give in to temptation. It's time to fill garden borders with marigolds, petunias, pelargoniums, ageratum, nemesia, lobelia, bacopa and the like.

Whether you're aiming for a sizzling display of hot and fiery reds, oranges and pinks (don't be afraid to clash colours), or the softer, paler pastels, or even the contrasting and traditional reds, whites and blues, now is the time to get them in.

You may have started to harden off greenhouse-grown bedding, ready for life outdoors. If you haven't, start straight away: keep plants outside during the day, and bring them in at night. After a few days, leave them outside in a sheltered place overnight as well. Then after a few more days they should be hardy enough to plant outside. This also applies to plug plants you may be sent from mail order nurseries, and plants you've bought from the garden centre. And keep a roll of fleece handy just in case of late frosts!

Buying bedding plants

■ CHOOSE PLANTS with few (or no) flowers. If they are in bloom while still on sale, you will have missed some of their season (and you'll end up paying a premium for them).

Also check their roots. Slip the plant out of its pot and make sure the roots are of an off-white colour – and there aren't too many or too few of them.

The cheapest plants are likely to be non-F1 hybrid petunias, marigolds, impatiens and nemesias.

Strong and vibrant hues

■ THE STRONGEST flower shades always come from the primary colours (red, blue and yellow), quickly followed by the secondary colours (green, purple and orange). Personal taste will dictate which you choose but, generally, using these colours will give you a striking border with a strong, vibrant feel.

Softer pastel shades

■ IN THE 1970s it became fashionable to use plants with pastel flowers (pinks, creams, pale blues, lavenders, and so on). These types of colour schemes remain the firm favourite with many gardeners. It is sometimes nice to also see an occasional or well-placed plant of a stronger colour for 'accent'.

Mixed 'fruit salad' colours

■ MANY GARDENERS just prefer an explosion of colour. This is often called the 'fruit salad effect', and it has its origins in the old-fashioned cottage garden style, where plants (usually perennials) of any colour were crammed into any space.

Keep summer bedding going

HAND WEEDING

■ CARRY THIS out on a weekly basis (at least) through the growing season. The sooner you remove them the better, as weeds compete for water, nutrients and rooting space.

FEEDING

■ A COUPLE of times throughout the growing season feed your bedding plants with a high-potash tomato fertiliser, to help keep the blooms coming.

WATERING

■ IN SUMMER the soil needs about an inch of water a week, depending on which plants are being grown. Push a finger 1in (2.5cm) into the soil and see if it is moist. If not, apply some water.

DEADHEADING

■ THIS SHOULD also be carried out once a week. Removing spent blooms keeps the display tidy, and stimulates plants to produce more flowers.

Step by step — How to plant up your summer beds and borders

1 Remove any spring bedding plants and weeds from the bed or border. Then it should be dug over, and a small handful of general fertiliser applied

2 Whether your bedding plants are home-sown or shop-bought, remove them from their pots or trays with care, so as not to damage them

3 The plants should be evenly spaced throughout the planting area: you can put the plants in place to get the right look before planting

4 Make sure the plants are well firmed in the soil, but not too hard (as this may damage the roots). Gently tug a leaf after planting – if the whole plant moves, it needs more firming

5 The final stage is to water the plants in. This is important as the soil can be quite dry at this time of year and, during transplanting, the roots will have been briefly exposed to the air

Anne's Family Garden

BEST SPOT
When our wisteria flowers I always try to find myself a job right alongside it, the better to enjoy its fabulous scented blooms

WISTERIA SINENSIS
This is the Chinese wisteria. Its natural habitat is moist woodland, but it's a classic choice for south and west facing house walls.

Wise words on wisteria

Anne basks in the glory of her wisteria and considers why some never quite make it

LAST SPRING everything in my garden flowered all at once, in a great crescendo of blossom. Even our wisteria was early. While it was in full bloom, I made sure I found a task right by it, all the better to enjoy those fragrant racemes of purplish buds and flowers.

The revolting collapsing terrace just in front (the site of the veranda of my dreams) had weeds poking through its slabs, so I set about removing them with a double-bladed gismo. Interestingly, some good plants such as dusty miller (*Lychnis coronaria*), aquilegias and good old Miss Willmott's ghost (*Eryngium giganteum*) have seeded themselves into the cracks, so I left them as camouflage.

I appreciate our wisteria for its willingness to flower abundantly, particularly as my mother used to have a nasty, spindly, mean wisteria in a very similar position (up against a south-facing house wall, with its roots squeezed into a gap in paving stones). Despite a lot of loving care, it resolutely refused to bloom and still hadn't when they moved away, 15 years after it had been planted!

Putting a finger on quite why some wisterias fail is tricky. Mum's was always spindly and few of its stems ever thickened up and matured. It could have done

"My mother used to have a nasty, spindly wisteria in a very similar position"

with more training out and formative pruning, but that's not the whole story.

It probably never found what it needed at the roots and was ever battling against house foundations and patio base. Ours must have been luckier and found better access to good soil.

Provenance is another factor. I expect our plant came from reliable stock, whereas when Mum's was planted back in the 1980's, when there seemed to be a lot of dodgy seedlings around.

Cuttings

The sea of white daisies from *Anthemis punctata* subsp. *cupaniana* is impressive after a somewhat ragged start in spring, proving what hardy, effective plants they are. I took a box of cuttings with a view to replacing them and every one has rooted, so I can start another patch now!

And the end of May is time to plant out bedding in beds and pots. This year I seem to have a random mix to choose from, including plants with pink, purple and white flowers such as heliotrope 'Princess Marina', *Nemesia* 'Berries and Cream' and verbena (all fragrant), plus a glowing pink dahlia with purple leaves, white fuchsia and ivy-leaved geranium.

Step by step — Planting a container for summer

GROWING MATTER
Place crocks over holes in the base and fill the container near to the top with potting compost. Arrange plants from the centre outwards

RIGHT HEIGHT
Ensure all plants are at the correct height in the pot, allowing a 1in (2.5cm) deep gap to the rim for watering. Fill in around them with compost

WATER IN
Using your fingers, firm the compost gently around the plants, and then water carefully, using a fine rose on the end of a watering can

Your gardening week

Ornamental garden

Summer lawn care

How can you keep grass looking in tip-top condition over the summer months?

WE ALL LIKE a lovely green lawn, and the height of summer is when we want it to look its best. Sadly, though, it's at this time of year when grass is under the most stress. To keep a lawn green, it needs a helping hand. Apart from the usual jobs of mowing, edging, and occasional watering there are other things you should be doing. Here are five ways to keep your turf in top condition.

Feeding:

■ IF YOUR LAWN has lost its vigour, spray on a liquid lawn feed (such as MiracleGro Water Soluble Lawn Food), using either a hose-end dilutor like this, or a watering can. Or scatter over 1oz per sq yd (15g per m2) sulphate of ammonia mixed with four times its weight in dry soil (to ensure even distribution and avoid scorching). Lightly brush in, then water this mixture. An organic option is to use chicken manure pellets. Repeat application if needed, but do not apply summer lawn feed after August as it contains too much nitrogen to use up ahead of the dormant season.

Aerating:

■ AREAS OF HEAVY footfall will become evident in dry weather – the ground becomes compacted, and grass growth is poor, lacklustre and there could even be bald patches starting to form. Pathways of browned grass can be improved by aerating (or spiking). This allows better air circulation and water intake to the root zone. A well-aerated lawn will manage better in periods of drought, too. Small areas can easily be spiked with a garden fork, spacing holes 4-6in (10-15cm) apart and the same deep.

Spot weeding:

■ EVEN IF you applied a combined lawn weed and feed product in spring, isolated broad-leaved weeds may still appear. It is better to spot-treat them with an appropriate selective lawn weedkiller spray (there are several ready-to-use types available). These kill the weeds with one application; the weeds die more quickly in bright sunlight.

Pest control:

■ CHAFER GRUBS (in late spring and early summer) and leatherjackets (the grubs of daddy-long-legs, in mid-summer to autumn) can be highly damaging to a lawn. They eat grass roots and cause yellow patches. Even worse, lawns are often ripped to pieces by birds that feed on them. Now is the time to water in a pesticide - Provado Lawn Grub Killer – to control them.

Watering:

■ IF YOU live in an area that has a hosepipe ban slapped on it – at any time of year – watering the lawn is illegal! Fortunately even in severely dry conditions the lawn is unlikely to die, it will just turn brown – roots below the soil should be fine and will produce fresh leaves when the rain returns. If you are allowed to water and the lawn needs it, do it thoroughly so the water penetrates deeply.

Step by step Repairing patches in the lawn

1 Use an old, sharp knife to cut out the section of turf that needs replacing. Lift the section and knock off excess soil back into the hole.

2 Sprinkle the area with a lawn seed and compost mix – about one handful of lawn seed to two handfuls of compost – or use a kit like MiracleGro Patch Magic.

3 Level and gently press down, then water in with a fine rosed watering can. Do not allow it to dry out. Avoid walking on the area until the new grass is well established.

Social climbers

Wisteria is often seen adorning the walls of chocolate-box homes, but as **Ian Hodgson** explains, this majestic climber has something to offer all gardeners

WISTERIA are rightly cherished for their heart-stopping cascades of springtime blossom. They make imposing features and although the most impressive specimens are often seen on stately homes or historic buildings, you don't have to be loaded to grow a wisteria. It's a climber that everyone can grow and I adore mine, which clambers up the front of my semi-detached house.

If wall space is a problem, don't dismiss wisteria, as I've seen them perform successfully in half barrels and large pots, and trained as standards, or along trellis in front gardens.

Wisterias always make a big statement, so choose your variety carefully. Flower colour ranges from pure white, through shades of lilac-pink and lavender-blue. Many are subtly bicoloured, or have a pronounced yellow blotch.

Named varieties are usually grafted – check your plant is actively growing above the graft union. If you can, buy when in flower to compare colour to the description on the label.

When planting, position the plant a foot away from the wall, lean the shoots in and secure to

Free-standing wisterias can be trained to grow like small trees in the border by initially supporting their stems with a wooden or metal framework structure

supports. Ensure there is sufficient room and depth of soil for roots to grow down and establish. Water in thoroughly, but do not feed with a nitrogen fertiliser. Too much feed won't encourage them to flower. If anything, mix in a slow release feed, high in potash, such as bonemeal. Plants grown in containers will also benefit from an annual dressing of fertiliser or refreshed compost.

Until established, keep young plants watered during prolonged dry weather. Don't plant right beside a door or window, but provide space into which the framework of shoots can expand.

You will need to create a robust framework to support the stems. Use a network of vine eyes screwed into the masonry, then strung with tensioned galvanised wire. If growing in pots or creating a freestanding bush you will need to use timber or metal on which to train the shoots.

Try white-flowered, scented Wisteria brachybotrys 'Shiro-kapitan' for something a little different

SIMPLE PRUNING

■ FOR THE FIRST YEAR or two after planting select and train strong leaders to create the main framework, shortening side shoots to two or three buds in late autumn. Once the required height is achieved, you can then prune back the leading shoot to encourage the top few side shoots to form the canopy.

Pruning has two purposes – first, to contain and direct growth of the plant, and second, to encourage flowering. The traditional practice is to cut back all new growth from mid-August to September by half, or to five buds, helping to create the short spurs on which flower buds form.

Tie in any strong growth you want to take higher or direct to new areas of wall, and thin out any spindly or crossing shoots. Rigorously remove growth encroaching on drainpipes, gutters or services.

Remove any shoots which appear at or below soil level.

Clusters of flower buds are produced at the base of the new shoots, so when leaves have fallen in late autumn or winter cut all the previously shortened shoots back to two buds.

However you grow and train it, wisteria is one of the most majestic performers you could ever plant. With just a little care they give their all year after year, and transform a bare wall into something really special.

5 TOP VARIETIES

1 W. FLORIBUNDA 'ALBA'
Elegant, white later-flowered variety, set against pale green leaves. Faint scent

2 W. FLORIBUNDA 'MULTIJUGA'
Classic long flowered variety, to 3ft (0.9m). Reasonable scent

3 W. FLORIBUNDA 'ROSEA'
Flowers lavender-pink, with yellow blotch. Delicate to good scent

4 W. SINENSIS 'AMETHYST'
Imposing lavender and dusky-pink bicolored flowers. Good scent

5 W. FRUTESCENS 'AMETHYST FALLS'
Flowers lilac blue, faintly scented. Flowers when in full leaf. Good for pots

SUPPLIERS

■ **Burncoose nursery, Cornwall**
✆ (01209) 860011
🖱 www.burncoose.co.uk

■ **Spring reach nursery, Surrey**
✆ 01483 284 769;
🖱 www.springreachnursery.co.uk

Your gardening week

Ornamental garden

How to grow tomatoes

Raise an early crop of tomatoes under glass

ONCE KNOWN as 'love apples', tomatoes are tender perennials, grown as annuals. The fruits come in many shapes and sizes, and colours including red, yellow and purple. Native to South America, when they arrived on British shores they were thought to be an aphrodisiac. Now they are popular in cooking worldwide.

Some tomato varieties such as 'Alicante' (pictured below) can be grown outdoors in a sunny, sheltered spot, but all will crop better when grown under cover in a greenhouse or polytunnel. Tomatoes contain lycopene which protects against cancers, as well as vitamins A and C.

Varieties to try

'**Ailsa Craig**' (Mr Fothergill's) Old favourite with excellent flavour.
'**Gardeners' Delight**' (T&M) Small fruits with a great flavour.
'**Rosada**' F1 (T&M) Well balanced acids & sugars for good taste.

Smartideas

When you break off a sideshoot (cordon types), dib it into a pot of moist cuttings compost and put it in a warm spot. It will soon take root, and can be grown on to crop later than the parent plant.

SIMPLE STEPS

WHEN TO SOW

■ START SOWING in January in a heated greenhouse, or early March in an unheated greenhouse.

HOW TO SOW

■ SOW A few seeds ¼in (6mm) deep in small pots or trays of moist seed compost (pic 1). Sprinkle compost or vermiculite lightly over the top, then place in a heated propagator at 15-30°C (59-86°F). Alternatively, put the pot in a clear plastic bag and stand it on a warm, bright windowsill indoors. When seeds germinate make sure you provide good ventilation.

PRICKING OUT

■ WHEN SEEDLINGS are big enough to handle, prick them out into small 3in (7cm) pots filled with John Innes No 2 or multipurpose compost (pic 2). Using a dibber, lift out the seedlings individually, holding each one by a leaf. Transplant them, one in each pot. Water well. Grow on in warmth and good light. The next job is to pot on, when necessary (pic 3).

ROUTINE CARE

■ GIVE PLANTS support, tying the stem to a cane or training up a string attached to the greenhouse roof (pic 4). Cordon types need their sideshoots, which grow between the main stem and leaf stems, pinching off (pic 5), when 1in (2.5cm) long. Feed plants once a week with high potash (tomato) liquid feed. Pinch out the main growing tip when six flower trusses have set.

HARVESTING

■ PICK FRUITS as soon as they colour up fully.

Cordon and bush tomatoes

■ VINE OR cordon tomatoes (also known as indeterminate) are grown on one single stem trained up a support. Sideshoots that grow between the main stem and the leaf axils are pinched out to stop branches growing. Do not pick off flower trusses which grow on the stem between two leaf axils. Bush (determinate) tomato varieties are allowed to grow side shoots and form a mound of straggly growth.

Common problems with tomatoes

Blossom end rot

■ SUNKEN DARK brown areas form at the base of swelling tomato fruits. This is caused by a lack of calcium, and is a result of irregular watering. Pick off affected fruits and instigate a very regular watering regime, several times a day if necessary.

Blight

■ THIS DESTRUCTIVE airborne fungus strikes in summer when the atmosphere is humid and the temperature high. Outdoor crops are most affected, but greenhouse crops can also suffer. Spray plants fortnightly with Bayer Fruit & Veg Disease Control from late May. Destroy affected plants. Some tomato varieties, such as 'Ferline' F1 from Thompson & Morgan, are said to be blight resistant.

Tomato moth caterpillar

■ THESE HUGE caterpillars usually strike the plants as they begin to crop in early summer. Leaves and fruit are eaten by fat green caterpillars up to 1½in (35mm) long. Track them down, pick them off and dispose of them.

Fruit splitting

■ FRUITS DEVELOP normally but just before being fully ripe, the skin splits open. The problem is caused by erratic swelling of the fruit – a result of erratic watering. Keep compost moist and water regularly. Affected fruits are fine to eat.

Gardener's tea break

WORDSEARCH

```
E R E Y A L Y A R T
E S D E E S Y P O O
M G U R E D P N T P
O N A O R R O A A C
Z I T A H I T E G U
I W H F S N F F A T
H O I I A I E A P T
R S V O N R N E O I
P I C K I N G L R N
D O O W D R A H P G
```

This word search contains names and words connected with plant propagation; these words are listed below. In the grid they may be read across, backwards, up, down or diagonally. Letters may be shared between words. Erroneous or duplicate words may appear in the grid, but there is only one correct solution. After the listed names are found there are 11 letters remaining; arrange these to make the **KEYWORD.**

CUTTING	KNIFE	RHIZOME
DIVISION	LAYER	SEED
GRAFT	LEAF	SOWING
GREENHOUSE	PICKING	TRAY
HARDWOOD	POT	
HARDY	PROPAGATOR	

SPOT THE DIFFERENCE

Here's *AG*'s Peter Seabrook (former *Gardeners' World* presenter and *The Sun*'s gardening editor), taking a well-earned break from gardening to enjoy a cuppa in his Essex garden. Can you spot the FOUR differences between these two pictures? (Answers can be found at the bottom of the page)

GOING POTTY

Mailbag

IT'S AMAZING what you can grow flowers in. I couldn't bare to throw my son's potty away, so as you can see I fill it every year with my favourite bedding plants!
Mr J Jozkow, Holyhead, Gwynedd

Problem solver
TOMATO BLIGHT

Q Douglas Simpson from Chepstow writes: "I've grown tomatoes under glass and outdoors for years. Last year the plants seemed healthy, until they started to develop blight, and it then rapidly destroyed them. I don't grow potatoes, nor do any of my neighbours, so what can I do to grow healthy tomatoes?"

A You can overcome blight by spraying plants with Bayer Fruit & Vegetable Disease Control, which is widely available from garden centres.
Outdoors you will have to repeat this treatment immediately if, after spraying, rain washes the fungicide from leaves (the important thing is to keep the leaves covered with a thin film of the fungicide).
Incidentally, the disease arrives when we have two consecutive days of comparative warmth and high humidity – conditions that are common in our British climate!

Quick tips

May
...more things to do

1 Sow your tender veg

■ CREATE SPACE in the greenhouse or on the windowsill to start off tender veg such as runner beans, French beans, courgettes, squashes and cucumber. For convenient potting on/planting out, sow individual seeds in cell trays filled with multipurpose compost.

2 Lift spring bedding plants

■ REMOVE SPRING bedding plants as they turn this month to make way for summer varieties. Place spent plants on the compost heap and prep soils. Apply a balanced fertiliser such as fish, blood and bone, turn over the soil and rake level. Allow time for soil to settle before re-planting next month.

3 Evening scent

■ ADD AN extra element to the late spring and summer garden by planting up pots of night-scented phlox (*Zaluzianskya capensis*) this month. Flowers will open in the evening to fill enclosed spaces with the scent of honey. Set out in free-draining soil or pot in multipurpose compost with added slow-release fertiliser.

4 Spring clean

■ AS YOU get the annual spring clean done in the home don't forget your houseplants. Clean leaves with a damp clean cloth. On tough spiky leaves use an old toothbrush and for delicate leaves use a soft brush. Removing dust allows your plants to photosynthesise at their optimum level, encouraging healthy growth through summer.

5 Protect tree fruit

■ APPLE AND pear trees can be affected by various fungal diseases. Two of the most common are scab and powdery mildew. May is a good month to apply a preventative spray such as Systhane Fungus Fighter. It is always best to apply it in late evening so you don't risk harming pollinating insects.

6 Plant summer bulbs

■ SUMMER FLOWERING bulbs can be safely planted through May with little risk of them rotting off. Common options include lilies, gladioli, tigridia, crocosmia and *Anemone* De Caen. All of these varieties prefer a sunny location. To aid drainage around the bulbs, add a little sand or grit to the planting hole before inserting the bulbs.

7 Peg strawberry runners

■ FOR OPTIMUM fruiting, strawberry runners should be removed from plants so energy is not wasted. But if you want to create new plants for free, retain a few runners on each plant and peg them into the soil. These will quickly root to make new young plants.

JUNE 2013

SATURDAY
1
GARDENING SCOTLAND, EDINBURGH

& BLOOM 2013, DUBLIN

SUNDAY
2
GARDENING SCOTLAND, EDINBURGH

& BLOOM 2013, DUBLIN

MONDAY
3
& BLOOM 2013, DUBLIN

TUESDAY
4

WEDNESDAY
5

THURSDAY
6

FRIDAY
7

SATURDAY
8

The RHS Garden at Wisley in Surrey, at 240-acres, is one of the UK's best-known ornamental and trials gardens

Visiting gardens

YOUR GARDEN will probably be looking at its very best this month. Plants are reaching maturity but not many have gone over, so growth is fresh and bright, lots of flowers are opening, and lots of crops in the veg plot are approaching harvest.

Which means it is also a great time to visit other people's gardens and enjoy them at their best. In the UK, we're spoilt for choice – from historic grand gardens of the National Trust, through the wonderful RHS demonstration gardens at Wisley, Hyde Hall, Rosemoor and Harlow Carr, to the private gardens opening for charity under the NGS Yellow Book scheme, and hundreds more besides. Visiting gardens is a great way to get ideas for your own plot, and to meet other keen gardeners. Many sell plants so you can stock up. And some of them even have wonderful tea shops – an unmissable treat!

Around 3,800 gardens around the UK open under the yellow book scheme. Find a copy at booksellers or visit www.ngs.org.uk

JUNE 2013

SUNDAY

9

MONDAY

10

TUESDAY

11

WEDNESDAY BBC GARDENERS' WORLD LIVE

12

THURSDAY BBC GARDENERS' WORLD LIVE

13

FRIDAY BBC GARDENERS' WORLD LIVE

14

SATURDAY BBC GARDENERS' WORLD LIVE

15

SUNDAY BBC GARDENERS' WORLD LIVE

16

Growing salad leaves

SALAD LEAVES are extremely easy and quick to grow. They are ideal for growing in pots or any kind of container indoors on a sunny windowsill, or outside. Growing your own salad leaves is also an excellent way to save money – much cheaper than buying mixed bags at the supermarket.

Salad leaves are full of goodness, from lutein for healthy eyesight, to folate to produce healthy red blood cells.

They're also easy to grow in containers. Fill the pot with multipurpose compost, water it well. Sprinkle your chosen mix of salad leaf seeds – which might include lettuce leaves as well as rocket, mustard and kale – thinly and evenly over the surface (spacing seeds about ½in/1cm apart). Cover them with a light sprinkle of dry compost and stand the pot on a bright windowsill, or in good light outside.

Seeds should germinate within a week, and be big enough to harvest in 3-4 weeks (when about 8in/20cm tall). Cut the leaves about 1in (2.5cm) above the compost, leaving the growing point intact; water and feed the pot, and you should get a second cutting about two weeks later.

Varieties to try

'Spicy Mix'
(Suttons) A spicy twist, ready in three weeks in summer

'Niche Oriental Mixed' (T&M) Ideal for containers

'Californian Mix' (Dobies) Mild-flavoured, ready in four weeks

JUNE 2013

MONDAY

17

TUESDAY

18

WEDNESDAY

19

THURSDAY

20

FRIDAY

21

SATURDAY

22

SUNDAY

23

MONDAY

24

Grow herbs on your kitchen windowsill

A BRIGHT KITCHEN windowsill is the ideal place to grow small pots of soft-leaved herbs, including basil, coriander and parsley. All thrive in the warm, moist atmosphere of a typical kitchen. They are quick growers and provide delicious flavouring for pasta and pizza, stir-fries and Asian dishes, as well as salads.

Fill two or three 3in (7cm) pots (or a larger one if you're a heavy herb user!) with multipurpose compost, firm down lightly, then water and allow to drain.

How to sow

Sow seeds of coriander or basil evenly over the surface, spacing seeds about ¼in (6mm) apart, then cover with a fine sprinkling of compost. Pop the pots in a clear plastic bag and place on the windowsill until seeds germinate.

Remove the bag and allow the herbs to grow on, keeping them watered as necessary, until they are large enough to cut – usually about six weeks from sowing. Sow pots every 2-3 weeks for a continuous supply through summer.

For parsley just sow about 10 seeds over the surface of the pot. Treat as above, but you can pick individual leaves for weeks from one pot, so resowing should be unnecessary, unless you use lots.

TUESDAY

25

WEDNESDAY

26

THURSDAY

27

FRIDAY

28

SATURDAY

29

SUNDAY

30

Pest and disease patrol

THE BEST way to stop pests and diseases damaging your plants is to identify and tackle any problems early. So whenever you're out in the garden, keep an eye out for trouble.

Go on a night time slug and snail hunt, armed with a torch and a bucket of salty water. You'll find lots of molluscs munching your plants under the cover of darkness – pick them up and drop them in the salty water to kill them, then put the bucket contents on the compost heap.

Aphids and fungi

The moment you see aphids in plant stems or flower buds, either rub them off or spray with a suitable contact or systemic pesticide.

Pick off plant leaves infected by brown spot fungus; if powdery mildew (like talcum powder dusted on leaves) strikes, water plants well and improve air circulation; downy mildew (like fine cotton wool on underside of leaves) is caused by too much moisture, so stop watering and improve air circulation.

Ornamental garden

Your gardening week

Wise watering

Will we be in for a hot summer in 2013? If so, you'll need to be sensible when watering

WATER IS ESSENTIAL to every living thing. Without it, neither you, nor any living plant or animal on this earth would survive. Over 90 per cent of a soft, herbaceous plant may consist of water. It is the water that keeps the soft young leaf and stem cells turgid, or plump and extended. But if water is in short supply this cell turgidity is lost so that the stems of herbaceous plants become limp, and

QUICK TIP

Water butts make sense – you can collect as much as 50,000 litres of rain per year from a house roof.

the leaves droop and wilt. Should a water shortage be prolonged, the plant will probably wither and die. So if there is a major demand for water this summer, you owe it to your plants – and your bank balance if you have a water metre – to conserve rainwater in a water butt and to use as little mains water as possible.

And this means you should be ultra-wise with your watering. On these pages are a few ideas that will certainly save you money, and may save your plants from wilting in the hot summer sun.

Drip irrigation systems

■ YOU CAN buy a complete drip-irrigation system. Pipes and branches of pipes with pre-drilled holes along their length can be laid throughout the area to be watered. They can be coiled and twisted to get close to specific plants – or, more accurately, the root area of specific plants. When they are connected to a mains tap or water store, the water seeps out of the holes and soaks the immediate area. This type of system is generally very efficient in its use of water. It's best to connect it to a timing device so it comes on at night.

Water retaining crystals and gels

■ WHEN PLANTING up containers you should mix into the compost polymer granules – known as 'water saving crystals' – which are widely available. Follow the directions on the packet. These dry granules absorb moisture, swelling to many times their own weight. They release moisture to plants over a long period. Some potting composts from garden centre contain granules or other wetting agents so check bags before you buy.

Using a sprinkler

■ A SPRINKLER can be very effective at delivering water to where it is needed. There are three basic designs: rotary, oscillating and hose. Rotary sprinklers throw water over a circular area up to 25ft (7.2m) across. Oscillating sprinklers (pictured) throw water over a square or rectangular area, which makes it easier to get water into a corner of the garden without drenching your neighbour! A sprinkler hose – a tube with tiny holes along one side – will water a narrow strip.

Although it will save you time, a sprinkler can waste water. Some water companies only allow the use of sprinklers if the household is on a metered water supply, but this differs around the country so check with your local board.

However, sprinklers are the sensible option for any closely planted areas, such as borders of perennials in full leaf, beds of thickly planted summer bedding, and lawns.

Make your sprinkler as water-efficient as possible by measuring the volume needed to provide sufficient water for the area. Spread jars around the garden. Time how long it takes to fill the jars to ½in (12mm) – the minimum water requirements of a lawn for the week. One inch (2.5cm) replaces all the water lost to the lawn during a week of no rain. Once you know how long to leave the sprinkler, on you can do away with the jars.

5 of the best drought tolerant garden plants

JERUSALEM SAGE
(*Phlomis fruticosa*)

ROCK OR SUN ROSE
(*Cistus x purpureus*)

BROOM
(forms of cytisus - pictured above)

LAVENDER
(forms of lavandula)

CENTURY PLANT
Agave americana 'Variegata'

Three ways to water more wisely

Soaking

■ DON'T BE fooled into thinking that, just because the soil surface is darker, that the area has been sufficiently watered. Plant roots detect even a small amount of surface water and grow towards it. So make sure you soak the area you're watering thoroughly, so it goes deep.

Grey water

■ BATH OR SHOWER WATER, once cooled, can be used on plants. It is possible to store such domestic water when rain water is no longer available. Ordinary household soaps – which are used in small quantity and heavily diluted – will not harm plants.

Don't use water from the toilet, or the waste from washing machines and dishwashers which use powerful chemical detergents. Do not use water from rinsing after cleaning a bath if a chemical cleaner was used.

Timing

■ IF YOU water plants during the heat of the day, much of it will evaporate, and do no good at all. Water droplets can also act as a magnifying glass when the sun is strong, and burn the plant – known as scorching. With the exception of lettuces (which can get mouldy) it is best to apply water in the evening or early morning when there is less chance of evaporation.

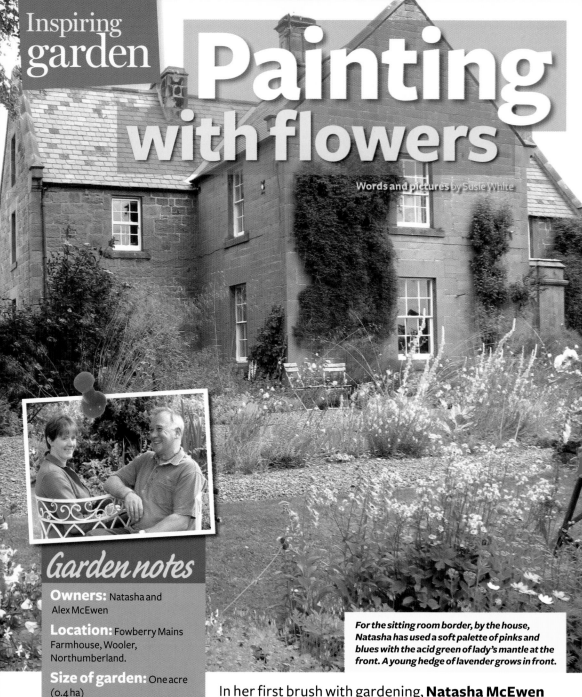

Painting with flowers

Words and pictures by Susie White

Garden notes

Owners: Natasha and Alex McEwen

Location: Fowberry Mains Farmhouse, Wooler, Northumberland.

Size of garden: One acre (0.4 ha)

Soil : Good, neutral loam enhanced with home-made compost and plenty of organic chicken manure pellets

Special features: Gravel beds with drought tolerant plants, colour themed borders with country style planting, vegetable garden, wild area under development.

Season visited: July

For the sitting room border, by the house, Natasha has used a soft palette of pinks and blues with the acid green of lady's mantle at the front. A young hedge of lavender grows in front.

In her first brush with gardening, **Natasha McEwen** has shown great artistic flair for planting up the Northumberland plot she shares with husband **Alex**

AS AN army wife, Natasha McEwen is no stranger to regularly moving home. It wasn't until she settled in a north Northumberland farmhouse with husband Alex and their three boys, that she discovered a talent for producing planting schemes as pretty as a picture.

When they moved in, the garden was bare, just waiting for someone with vision to transform it, and with Alex now working locally for a barristers' chambers, the couple were able

Natasha has planted a hot border against the boundary drystone wall. The landscape beyond is one of gently undulating hills, hedges and fields of sheep. Perennials, such as Centaurea dealbata, a lovely purple knapweed, are combined with self-seeding annuals.

to devote time to creating their first garden together.

"I think of it as painting with flowers," says Natasha. "I use my hands to 'frame' the view of groups of plants, outlining 'paintings' to see if I want to change things. I spend my whole time moving plants around – six inches to the left here, or further forward there, just to get it right." And now, after nine years, she feels she has the garden mostly as she wants it.

While Alex does the heavy work, Natasha is able to give her full attention to the planting and colour schemes. Among them is a border by the house, 'the sitting-room border', with its subtle palette of pinks and blues, echoed and developed in two expansive curving beds further

away from the house. These form half of a large circle, the other half made from a 7ft (2.1m) tall hawthorn hedge. Then, at the heart of it, is an inner circle of blue lupins and alliums surrounded by whitebeam.

Around the base of three old fruit trees there are meandering paths, amongst planting that is strong on foliage. Large variegated hostas jostle with the striped grass known as 'gardener's garters', by a tiny

The Mediterranean style planting contrasts in a subtle way with the Northumbrian landscape beyond. "I've learnt so much from my own garden and am now doing planting plans and consultancy work, helping other people create their gardens," says Natasha.

Tall grasses create a gently swaying latticework through which the house is glimpsed. The feathery plumes of Stipa gigantea on the left combine beautifully with orange yarrow. To the right, the purple tinged plumes of calamagrostis are perfect with purple sage and the unusual half-hardy Berkheya purpurea, a showy thistle-like plant with pale mauve daisy flowers.

As the foliage borders under the old fruit trees emerge from the shade, they give way to more sun-loving plants such as this vibrant Cistus purpureus. This is a Mediterranean shrub that needs dry conditions. It has crimson flowers with deep central blotches and vivid yellow stamens.

Below: 'Rosa Mundi', a Gallica rose known from before the 16th century. It's said to be named after fair Rosamund, the mistress of Henry II and is a play on the words 'Rose of the world'. Other roses grow here are 'Redouté' for its lovely scent, as well as 'Tuscany Superb', and 'Buff Beauty'.

This simple wooden bridge spans a boggy area near old fruit trees. The graceful spires of Ligularia przewalskii rise above attractive serrated leaves, against a background of roses and the striped grass Phalaris arundinacea 'Picta' (gardener's garters).

Cirsium rivulare 'Atropurpureum': This lovely thistle stands tall above its foliage in a border that is predominately pink, red and white. As its species name suggests, it likes moist soil (rivulare means 'growing by a stream'). When flowers fade stems need cutting right back under the foliage to encourage a second flush of these gorgeous wine-red thistles.

pond. Yellow spires of *Ligularia przewalskii* and handsome rheum leaves lap against a lichen-encrusted bridge.

A 'Seagull' rose with open, white flowers, scrambles up one of the old trees.

But it is in the area in front of the house that Natasha's artistic talent has really come to the fore. Having gravelled the wide drive that leads to the front door the couple were horrified at the dauntingly severe effect. "In the end we decided to block off the entrance with large stones and send cars around the back of the house instead," says Natasha.

This then gave her full rein to break up the expanse of gravel with suitable plants.

Taking her inspiration from the planting in her mother's courtyard garden in France, as well as Beth Chatto's gravel garden in Essex, Natasha has created a flowing design of drought tolerant plants without the boundary constraints of a traditional border.

A weaving path leads to the front door through arching stems of *Stipa gigantea*, scented evening primroses, tall lemon yellow mulleins, lambs' ears, thyme and sweet smelling dianthus. Lady's mantle froths over the edges of the gravel, while cosmos stand in pots by the front door. It's a welcome that delights the senses – and it's a picture-perfect scene.

Your gardening week

Semi-ripe cuttings

Make new plants from the fresh growth on shrubs and woody perennials

Take cuttings in the morning, with a knife or secateurs

NOW IS the time to propagate shrubs, climbers and woody herbs from semi-ripe cuttings. This is one of the easier cuttings techniques and can be done from now until mid-October, taking stems of this season's growth.

The cuttings are called 'semi-ripe' because the new growth hasn't had time to fully ripen – the base will be harder and turning woody, whereas the tip will be lush and soft because it is still actively growing.

To take cuttings you'll need a clean, sharp pair of secateurs or knife, a clear plastic bag, a few 3in (7cm) pots or a modular tray, and some gritty seed and cutting compost. Adding horticultural grit (about a third by volume) will improve drainage and the chances of the cuttings striking.

Fill the pots or trays with the compost, give them a good water and allow to drain before setting cuttings in them.

Take the cuttings early in the morning before the sap begins to rise. Make sure you don't take them on a very windy day, and choose plants that are in good condition – free of pests and diseases and healthy (this will be indicated by lush, green leaves and not drooping). Work quickly to avoid the cuttings wilting.

The warm temperatures of summer help the stems to root quickly, without the use of propagators, but to get good results they will root more reliably if kept in a greenhouse or coldframe.

Check the cuttings regularly after three months. When roots appear through the base of the pot, pot the cuttings on into individual pots filled with John Innes No 2.

Step by step

Leaf size determines the way you take your cuttings. For plants with average sized leaves like this *Choisya ternata* or Mexican orange, follow this simple step-by-step:

1 Using a sharp knife or secateurs cut a strong and healthy shoot about 8in (20cm) long from the current season's growth, just above a node (where leaves meet the stem)

2 Remove the soft top 2in (5cm) cutting just above a pair of leaves, then trim the cutting so that it's 4-6in (10-15cm) long, cutting just below a node at the base. Take off lower leaves (leave 2 - 4 leaves)

3 Dip the base of the cutting into a rooting compound, shaking off the excess. Push the base of the cutting into a modular tray or 3in (9cm) pot of filled with good, moist seed and cuttings compost

Large-leaved plant cuttings

■ To increase your stocks of large-leaved plants such as fatsia (pictured), fig and hydrangea successfully you'll need to reduce the leaf size. This will help to reduce the amount of water lost and in turn will give the cutting more energy to root.

■ Cut a young, vigorous shoot just below a node (pic 1).

■ Now remove all of the lower leaves plus the soft top of the stem, and cut down the one top leaf you've left to about half its original size (pic 2).

■ Make a 1mm deep cut on the side of the stem, at the base, dust the base and the wound with rooting compound then insert the stem deeply, up to 1in (2.5cm) below surface in cuttings compost (pic 3).

Taking cuttings from small-leaved plants

■ Semi-ripe cuttings can be used to propagate plants with small leaves such as whipcord hebe, heather (pictured), tamarix, rosemary, perovskia and most conifers. Select a healthy shoot, 3-5in (7.5-13cm) long, from this year's growth (left). Remove leaves from the bottom 1in (2.5cm) of the stem using your thumb and forefinger then dip the base in rooting compound. Insert the cuttings 1in (2.5cm) deep (right) into pots or modules filled with seed and cuttings compost. Set conifer cuttings 1/2in (1cm) deep.

Aftercare of cuttings

■ Your cuttings will take between six months and a year to root well. Water if the compost is dry and remove any yellowing leaves. In the spring harden off the cuttings. In May or June the cuttings can be potted up singly (right) into John Innes No2 or multipurpose compost, or planted out in a nursery bed. Move to final planting position in autumn.

Hormone rooting compound

■ Hormone rooting compound helps cuttings to make roots quicker. It comes in a gel or powder but both do the same job.

Try taking cuttings from these plants

Climbers:

- Campsis
- Ivy
- Honeysuckle
- Jasmine
- Hydrangea petiolaris
- Passionflower
- Solanum

Herbs:

- Bay
- Sage
- Lavender
- Thyme
- Rosemary

Shrubs:

- Abelia
- Camellia
- Berberis
- Ceanothus
- Buddleja
- Choisya
- Buxus

Trees:

- Arbutus
- Elm
- Cercis
- Larch
- Hazel
- Picea

Kitchen garden

Your gardening week

How to grow
courgettes and squashes

These Mediterranean vegetables make a tasty addition to stews, stir-fries and barbecues

FROM TINY green or yellow skinned courgettes just 4in (10cm) long, to pumpkins weighing three-quarters of a ton and weird alien-looking fruits, the squash family is astonishing. For eating, the best are the sweet tasting butternut squash, and the delicate fleshed courgette. They're good for you, too, packed with vitamins A, C, potassium, manganese, and vitamin E. Courgettes are at their best when harvested young. Cutting them will encourage more to grow. In contrast winter squashes should be cut from the vine late in the season and ripened on a warm windowsill before cooking or storing the fruits.

Varieties to try

Courgette 'Satelite'
F1 (DT Brown) Ball shaped fruits

Winter squash 'Harrier'
F1 (T&M) Butternut type, big fruits (pictured)

Courgette 'Atena' F1 (Suttons) Tasty, yellow, thin-skinned fruits

SIMPLE STEPS

SITE & SOIL
■ A WARM, sheltered, sunny site with deep, moist soil which is neutral to slightly acid. Dig in lots of well-rotted manure or garden compost in the autumn before planting. Rake in a balanced fertiliser such as growmore before sowing/planting.

WHEN TO SOW
■ NOT TOO early! In pots in the greenhouse (pic 1) from mid- to late April to harden off and plant out in mid-May, or direct in the soil from early to mid-June.

SOW UNDER GLASS
■ SOW SEEDS singly in 3in (7cm) pots filled with a good quality multipurpose compost. Set seeds about 1/2in (12mm) deep. Water well and place in a heated propagator, or in a plastic bag on a warm windowsill; the ideal temperature is 20-25°C (68-77°F). After germination ventilate well and grow on in good light. Keep the compost moist. Harden off plants to set out in mid-May.

SOW IN THE SOIL
■ WATER THE prepared soil well, then sow two seeds per 'station' or growing position, 1in (2.5cm) deep. Stations should be 3ft (90cm) apart each way. Cover with a jam jar until after germination. If

Smart ideas

Sow courgettes a couple of seeds at a time, every three weeks until early June for a succession of crops through until the first frost of autumn.

both seeds germinate at each station, remove the weakest.

ROUTINE CARE
■ WATER REGULARLY (pic 2), then mulch. Cut off withered leaves.

HARVEST
■ PICK FRUITS of courgettes young (pic 3) to encourage more fruit to set. Leave winter squashes as long as possible.

Quick tips

June ...more things to do

1 Camellia care

■ NOW THAT the flowering season for camellias is over, and next year's flower buds are about to form, it's time to pay them a little attention. Feed plants with an ericaceous fertiliser or specialist camellia feed, water plants well and, if necessary, cut stems back to keep the plant within bounds.

2 Water new lawns

■ ALTHOUGH IT is not politically correct to water lawns (they always re-grow after a drought) make an exception with new grass. Whether recently sown or turfed, new grass will need watering in dry weather. If you don't do it, the young seedlings will scorch and dry up, and turf will curl at the edges.

3 Trim topiary

■ TOPIARY BOX balls, pyramids and other shapes should be in need of a trim to keep their shape. Derby Day (2 June) is the traditional day to get this done. If yours covers a wire frame, use shears to snip back to the wire. Go cautiously if 'free styling': cut in small stages and regularly step back to look at your work from afar.

4 Mower settings

■ IF YOU'VE been mowing the lawn regularly for several weeks, you should now be able to set mower blades at their lowest setting. However, if your lawn has been parched by a lack of rain it may be best to set a cutting height no lower than 1in (2.5cm).

5 Thinning apples

■ MANY LITTLE fruits fall off apple trees during June. Don't worry, it's normal. There may still be too many. If you want larger fruits, thin out each remaining cluster by removing the central 'king fruit'. This won't grow properly anyway, and leaves the others room to develop well.

6 Dividing irises

■ LARGE CLUMPS of bearded and rhizome iris can be lifted and divided six weeks after flowering. Lift clumps and cut off healthy rhizome pieces that each have leaves attached. Reduce leaves by half, and replant 6in (15cm) apart in a sunny spot.

7 Controlling couch grass

■ COUCH GRASS is a perennial weed with wiry, underground stems and creeping shoots. It is essential to kill the roots. Dig out every piece of root, or spray leaves with glyphosate weedkiller such as Roundup.

JULY 2013

MONDAY

1

TUESDAY

2

WEDNESDAY

3

THURSDAY

4

FRIDAY

5

SATURDAY

6

SUNDAY

7

MONDAY

8

Sow foxgloves

F OXGLOVES ARE biennials. These plants make foliage growth in their first year and flower in the next. They're hardy and very easy to grow from seed (and very expensive to buy as plants from garden centres). Sown now, and overwintered in a cold frame or greenhouse they'll be ready to put on a fantastic display next spring.

1 Fill a small pot with soil-based John Innes seed compost, firm it lightly, water and allow to drain. Mix the tiny foxglove seeds with a pinch of dry sand and scatter the mixture evenly over the compost. Pop the pot in a clear plastic bag and place it on a warm, bright windowsill out of direct sunlight.

2 When seeds germinate remove the plastic bag and grow on the seedlings until large enough to handle, then prick them out into large cell trays or small, individual pots filled with John Innes No 1 compost. Grow on in a cold frame outdoors. Set them out in their flowering positions in early spring.

JULY 2013

TUESDAY

9

RHS HAMPTON
COURT PALACE
FLOWER SHOW

WEDNESDAY

10

RHS HAMPTON
COURT PALACE
FLOWER SHOW

THURSDAY

11

RHS HAMPTON
COURT PALACE
FLOWER SHOW

FRIDAY

12

RHS HAMPTON
COURT PALACE
FLOWER SHOW

SATURDAY

13

RHS HAMPTON
COURT PALACE
FLOWER SHOW

SUNDAY

14

RHS HAMPTON
COURT PALACE
FLOWER SHOW

MONDAY

15

TUESDAY

16

Declare war on weeds!

THERE ARE few more important jobs in the garden than weeding. Once they take hold weeds grow quickly, stealing moisture and nutrients and swamping the growth of the garden plants you want to thrive. The key to successful weeding is to do it regularly, tilling through the soil around your plants with a hoe just skimming beneath the surface to chop the heads off emerging seedlings.

Hoeing is best done when the soil surface is dry, when the weeds will shrivel up and vanish. In wet weather it's more effective (but slower) to hand weed with a small fork, carefully lifting the weeds with their roots out of the soil and composting them. Avoid composting weeds that have flowered and set seed – bin or burn these as the seed can survive in the compost until the following year.

Tough, deep rooted perennial weeds like couch grass, bindweed, dandelion or ground elder are best dug out, roots and all. Alternatively treat them with a systemic weedkiller containing glyphosate. – applied very carefully!

JULY 2013

WEDNESDAY

17

THURSDAY

18

FRIDAY

19

SATURDAY

20

SUNDAY

21

MONDAY

22

TUESDAY

23

WEDNESDAY RHS TATTON PARK
FLOWER SHOW

24

Prune wisteria

A WISTERIA IN full bloom in May is a magnificent sight. If you've chosen the right place to grow yours, and follow some simple pruning rules, it'll be the envy of your neighbours for years to come.

By this stage of the year wisteria should have lots of long, green stems coming off its main framework of woody stems. To encourage good flowering next spring, cut these new stems right back to 6in (15cm) from their points of origin on the main stem (pictured below) – leave about three leaves on the cut stem. Make the cut just above a bud or leaf.

If you want to extend the wisteria further one or two of the new stems can be tied onto the wires or support.

Pruning out the new growth improves air circulation around stems and leaves – which helps to keep mildews and moulds at bay. It also allows more sunlight in to ripen the remaining growth and boost flower bud production.

In February you can boost flowering more by cutting back growth from the main stems even harder.

> **QUICK TIP**
> New wisteria may be too young to bloom – these plants can take seven years before they flower reliably

JULY 2013

THURSDAY
RHS TATTON PARK
FLOWER SHOW
25

FRIDAY
RHS TATTON PARK
FLOWER SHOW
26

SATURDAY
RHS TATTON PARK
FLOWER SHOW
27

SUNDAY
RHS TATTON PARK
FLOWER SHOW
28

MONDAY
29

TUESDAY
30

WEDNESDAY
31

Summer care of garden roses

Pests and diseases
■ Roses are prone to aphid attack, and blackspot disease. Spray plants in mid spring and again in midsummer with Rose Clear or a similar combined insecticide/fungicide.

Feeding
■ Roses benefit from three feeds per year. A balanced fertiliser or specialist rose fertiliser – 2oz per sq yd (65g per m) – will encourage more blooms. Feed plants up to the end of July, no later.

Dead-heading
■ The first flush of flowers will be over by now, and the sooner the dead blooms are removed the better. Cut down the flowered stem by about one third. However you should not dead-head roses grown for their autumn display of hips.

Remove suckers
■ Suckers come from below the rose graft union (this is visible as a swelling near the base of the rose stem). They do not appear on roses grown on their own roots, such as species roses. Suckers frequently have greater vigour than the main plants and, if left, will take over. They will not, however, have the same traits as the main plant (note different leaf size and shape, right), and rarely flower. Remove as soon as they are seen. Remove a sucker with a knife or a pair of secateurs, severing it at the point where it joins the rootstock below the graft – it may be necessary to scrape some soil away to see where this is.

Watering
■ Roses are reasonably drought tolerant, but there are occasions when summer watering is a must. If we get a particularly long, dry spell make sure you water any newly-planted roses and any plants sheltered by a wall or fence.

Your gardening week

Seasonal jobs in the greenhouse

Summer heat and sunshine need careful management if plants are to benefit fully

Feeding & watering

■ WITH VIGOROUS growth and swelling fruits, all greenhouse crops will benefit from careful watering. Too much is as bad as too little, but the compost about an inch below the surface should always be moist. If it's not, water well. Feed all fruiting plants every two weeks with a high potash (tomato) liquid fertiliser.

1 Damping down

■ A GREENHOUSE in summer can get very hot, and plants growing inside can lose water very quickly. You can slow down the process by keeping the humidity up. Soak the floor and all other hard surfaces (this should include the glass) with water. This will help to prevent plants from getting stressed by heat.

3 Shading plants

■ TOO MUCH bright sunlight can cause scorching of plant leaves, as well as wilting and stress. Blinds, greenhouse paint products (these will turn transparent in the rain) and netting all provide useful shade. You could even think about growing tall plants nearby to act as a natural sun barrier. Fleece (pictured) is an easy option.

4 Pest control

■ JULY IS THE MONTH when greenhouse whitefly can infest at a rapid rate. Spray with a contact insecticide or use the biological control Encarsia formosa. This parasitic wasp lays it eggs in the whitefly larvae. These then hatch from within, killing the whitefly. As this is a live product you cannot usually buy it over the counter, but many garden centres will order for you, or contact Defenders www.defenders.co.uk Tel: 01233 813121.

5 Ventilation

■ AIR CIRCULATION in a greenhouse is important to keep temperatures down, and to avoid fungal disease promoted by humid, static air. For good air movement, a greenhouse should have an opening on both sides of the roof, and louvre vents near the bottom. In summer all vents should be open so that warm air can be replaced by cooler air coming in at the base. It may be necessary to leave the door open on very hot days. However if you grow tomatoes and there is a risk from tomato blight, reduce ventilation to prevent the airborne spores from entering the greenhouse.

6 Pinching out

■ MOST OF US have tomatoes in our greenhouses. To keep productivity up, regularly pinch out the sideshoots from cordon tomatoes (pictured below). Sideshoots grow from the point where the leaf stems joins the main stem. Pinching out concentrates energy on fruit development. Also remove some lower leaves to improve air circulation and boost fruit ripening.

7 Harvest crops

■ TO ENJOY GREENHOUSE crops at their best it is essential to harvest them as soon as they are ripe. Tomatoes, cucumbers, aubergines, chillies and many other early sown vegetables will be ripening. Picking the fruits as soon as they reach maturity will encourage more to set, increasing the crop. Fruits left on the plants will quickly go past their best, and the plant will stop producing.

8 Deal with disease

■ TWO COMMON PROBLEMS in greenhouses are powdery mildew and downy mildew caused by insufficient watering (powdery mildew) and excessive watering or high humidity and lack of air circulation (downy mildew), the latter pictured here on aubergine flowers. To beat these problems water regularly but not excessively, ensure good air circulation, pick off affected bits of the plant, and in severe cases spray with a suitable fungicide such as Bayer Fruit & Vegetable fungus fighter.

Anne's Family Garden

PLEASURE NOT PAIN
We've battled deer and rabbits to arrive at the point where cutting roses is a pleasure.

Anne Swithinbank

Blooms for a birthday

Birthday girl **Anne** makes sure she has plenty of gorgeous flowers for cutting

THIS IS my birthday month, and these days I'm cheap to please, because we can fill the house with my favourite flowers from the garden. This was not always so, partly because we've had to introduce the likes of peonies, roses and iris and take the time to sow and grow annuals like sweet peas, love-in-a-mist and cornflowers.

I've also had to overcome my aversion to harvesting flowers as though they were crops. It's all very well to think of cutting them in bud or bloom as early dead-heading, but to me it used to seem like robbing my plants of their crowing glory.

First, I had to plan the rose border with cutting in mind, which meant choosing varieties with long stems, and setting three of one kind together for a plentiful supply.

The peonies were sited a long way from the house, so I can't see their flowers anyway without going for a walk. More transient flowers for cutting are raised in rows in the kitchen garden, so they look business-like and there for a purpose.

Now I'm totally in the swing of it and love nothing better than roaming about the place, cutting here and there to gather a colourful, fragrant and sometimes eccentric bouquet.

I recently gathered a selection of roses: the yellow 'Graham Thomas', dusky 'Pegasus', peachy 'Crown Princess Margareta' and deep red 'William Shakespeare'. Taking them from the rose garden hardly showed; there were plenty of blooms left behind, making their own frothy combination with the globe heads of alliums (*Allium christophii* has taken over from *A.* 'Purple Sensation') and the long mauve spikes of catmint 'Walker's Low'.

Soon I'll be working my way through the rose bed, removing dead heads and, after a shower when the soil is moist, delivering another dressing of slow-release fertiliser to the plants. I don't spray against diseases like black spot, mildew and rust but try to keep them strong and healthy instead.

Filling gaps

Having lost many tender plants to the recent cold winters, we've been going around filling gaps with bedding plants, either sown from seed or grown from bought-in seedlings. I opted for hardy kinds, as we no longer heat the greenhouse.

Antirrhinums, clarkia and annual phlox have settled down well and will fill these beds with much-appreciated summer colour.

Three floral summer gap fillers

CLARKIA AMOENA
Used to be called godetia. Bushy plants are so covered in bloom (usually pink or mauve) you can hardly put a pin between them.

ANTIRRHINUMS
A good mix of these will bring an entire sweetshop of flower colours to your borders. I love the shapely spikes, too.

ANNUAL PHLOX
This is the first time in years that I've grown *Phlox drummondii,* and I'm really enjoying the character and flowers of the plants.

Gardener's tea break

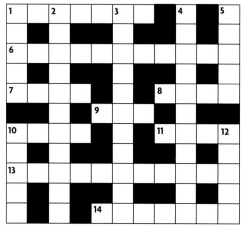

CROSSWORD...

just for fun Answers below

|1| |2| |3| |4| |5|
6						
7				8		
		9				
10				11		12
13						
		14				

ACROSS

1 Popular hardy and tender shrub, frequently used in patio containers, hanging baskets and as pot plants (7)
6 A long hosepipe made up with lots of shorter pipes will have one or more of these! (11)
7 Common name for, and the fruit of, *Prunus spinosa* (4)
8 Insects that secrete formic acid (4)
9 Common name for any plant of the hedera genus (3)
10 You do this to a plant when you transplant it, say from one part of the garden to another (4)
11 Space enclosed by the threads of a net; a small one is needed to protect cabbages from butterflies, for example (4)
13 Blooming plants that are attractive and, to some, weeds! (11)
14 Genus of evergreen shrubs and trees, of the protea family, and grown for their flowers and foliage (7))

DOWN

1 The rubber plant and fig genus (5)
2 The bindweed genus (11)
3 Genus of late spring- or summer flowering perennials, suitable for rock gardens and borders (11)
4 Royal regalia of state, and a cultivar of Regal pelargonium (5,6)
5 Little cylinders of soil left, usually on the lawn, by earthworms (5)
10 You should brush away 5 down, before cutting the lawn with this! (5)
12 Popular soft, leafy perennial, also known as the plantain lily (5)

SPOT THE DIFFERENCE

Chris Beardshaw, the BBC Radio 4 Gardeners' Question Time panellist, made his name as Channel 4's Flying Gardener, and through appearances on BBC2's Gardeners' World. But can you spot the FOUR differences between these pictures of Chris in a tropical garden at the RHS Chelsea Flower Show? (Answers can be found at the bottom of the page)

GOING GREEN

Mailbag

MY WIFE and I wanted a 'green' roof on our shed, but felt it was too expensive. Then she suggested we create shallow wooden 'planters' filled with sedums and alpines instead. We used tantalised batten for the edges, screwed directly to the roof. I've added a bead of silicone to prevent water leakage. Then we filled them with a mix of potting compost and vermiculite dressed with flint chippings to weigh it down.
Stephen Gaulter, Malmesbury

Problem solver

Q Helen Brown from Norbury, London writes: "My neighbour's cats always foul my garden. The smell can be awful. How can I stop them?"

A You could try one of the various cat repellents on the market, but not everyone rates them. Avoid leaving bare patches of soil – plant densely. Grow the curry plant (*Helichrysum italicum*), and the scaredy-cat plant (*Coleus canina*), both of which cats dislike.

Enjoy cut flowers indoors

THERE IS nothing to beat a bouquet of flowers picked fresh from the garden, especially if you've grown them yourself! But cut flowers can go over quickly, lasting only a couple of days in some cases. Some last longer than others. Sturdy-stemmed blooms, such as alstroemerias, carnations, delphiniums, lilies, roses and sunflowers can last in a vase for up to 14 days. But all cut flowers can be helped to look their best for longer. Here are a few ideas to help:

QUICK TIP
Don't use softened water for cut flowers (if you use a water softener) as this contains sodium, which will spoil them. Use bottled water instead

Selecting stems
■ Stems cut from large plants producing stiff-stemmed flowers will last longest. Pick from vigorous plants that have no sign of pests or disease. The stems shouldn't be slimy, broken or drooping, and the blooms should be just opening or soon to open.

Cutting stems
■ Cut the stems you select with a sharp pair of clean secateurs. Cut cleanly, just above a leaf or bud. Immediately place the cut stem into a deep pail of cold water. The water should come at least half way up the stem.

Display flowers
■ Keep the cut stems cool and in the shade while preparing the water and vase. The vase should be clean and free of mould or algae. Fill it with clean water and add cut flower food. Now remove any leaves from the flower stems that would sit below the water's surface, and cut 1in (2.5cm) off the bottom of the stem just before placing them into the water.

Keep you cut flowers happy
■ Keep the vase in a light place, but out of direct sunlight and drafts. Change the water every two days to stop it going stagnant, and cut a further 1in (2.5cm) from the bottom of each stem every time the water is changed. Pick off flowers that fade, and remove drooping or damaged leaves.

Take care
■ Lily pollen is poisonous to cats and it can easily rub off onto their fur. The pollen can also stain clothing permanently. As soon as the flowers of lilies open, wearing rubber gloves, use scissors to carefully cut out the stamens of each flower and bin them.

Heady
hydrangeas

Holehird Gardens in Cumbria is home to an amazing 303 types of hydrangea, and is a dream true for lovers of this summertime shrub

There are more colourful and shapely hydrangea varieties than you could ever have dreamed of, says **Neil Ross**

HYDRANGEAS REMIND me of childhood holidays. With loud colours reminiscent of either candyfloss or azure summer skies, they are mixed up in my memories of favourite seaside trips along with ice creams, donkey rides and banks of fuchsia and montbretia. Fat and fun, yes – but sophisticated?

Well, when I was on a short break in the Lake District I discovered another side to these easy summer performers: beautiful peeling bark, the promise of autumn colour, and exciting colours and flower shapes belonging to varieties I hadn't come across before.

Just up the hill from Windermere, Holehird Gardens is home to the Lakeland Horticultural Society, and its 15 acres contain the National Hydrangea Collection.

Hydrangeas are easy shrubs to get along with – apart from the tricky Japanese names, which require some serious brain training. The collection is largely propagated from easy-to-take soft tip cuttings, and this maintains the range of varieties reliably.

There are three main species of hydrangea. The large, brightly coloured macrophylla types are the best known, and are categorised into round-headed mopheads or 'hortensias', and the more dainty, flatheaded 'lacecaps'.

The mophead I remember from my holidays is 'Générale Vicomtesse de Vibraye' – a stalwart of seaside resorts with its plump mounds of candyfloss-coloured flowers.

Hydrangeas pack a punch just at the point our gardens are in need of a new injection of colour

The subtle-looking Hydrangea serrata, however, is usually of lacecap form. Originating from woodland and mountain regions, this species is much hardier than its bustier seaside cousin and is easier to prune. Most macrophylla varieties flower on two-year-old growth, and in harsh winters they lose their flowering wood. Serrata types flower on fresh growth so

Paniculata hydrangeas have lovely cone-shaped flowerheads. If left unpruned they grow into large shrubs. Prune hard in spring to keep them compact

no matter how bad the weather or how clumsily we chop them, they bloom regardless.

Hydrangea paniculata – another oriental favourite – also flowers on new wood, and is reliably hardy and easy to prune.

Paniculata hydrangeas make huge cones of white flowers, which sometimes fade to attractive tints – they are becoming increasingly popular.

All forms of hydrangea suffer from few pests and diseases, and are easy to care for. An annual prune – taking out a third of the oldest growth to the base – a good mulch and a handful of general fertiliser is all the care most of the collection needs.

Holehird Gardens are open all year
✆ (01539) 446008
www.holehirdgardens.org.uk

'Générale Vicomtesse de Vibraye' has clear pink mophead flowers that blue well in acid soils

HOW TO GROW HYDRANGEAS

PLANT in a well-drained but moisture-retentive soil rich in organic matter, and remember to water well in summer

PROTECTION from hot midday sun will stop flowers fading and leaves scorching

YELLOW leaves are often a sign of nitrogen deficiency, so try watering the roots with ammonium sulphate, which also acts to acidify the soil

ALTHOUGH it's a myth that last year's spent flowers protect hydrangea bushes from frost, you should wait until early spring to prune as swelling buds will show you where best to cut back to

OLD and ungainly shrubs are best rejuvenated by cutting everything down to the ground and starting again

FEED hydrangeas in spring, using a good-quality general fertiliser

IF you garden on alkaline soil and want blue hydrangeas, grow in a pot of ericaceous compost and add aluminium sulphate every spring

HYDRANGEA SUPPLIERS
www.ashwoodnurseries.com
✆ (01384) 401996

www.millcottageplants.co.uk
✆ (01749) 676966

Your gardening week

How to grow
runner beans

Picked young, fresh from the plant, runner beans offer superb flavour and texture

WHATEVER THE size of your garden, make room for some runner beans. They usually produce a heavy crop of succulent pods, and they look great. The Victorians originally grew runners as ornamental climbing plants.

The flowers, in white, red, soft pink, or a mixture, look pretty so you could grow them in the flower border up a rustic frame. These twining climbers – you don't need to tie them to supports, they'll wrap themselves tightly around bamboo canes or hazel stakes – will grow 8-10ft (2.7 – 3m) tall so pick your spot carefully, and provide a wigwam or row of supports about 7ft (2.1m) tall. If you're sowing beans in pots under cover from mid April, for an early crop, you must 'harden off' plants just before setting them out in the soil when the weather warms. Stand the pots outdoors in the sunshine during the day, and bringing them back under cover at night. Do this for 7-10 days, then the plants will be ready to stay out.

Runner beans suffer from few problems. Black aphids can colonise the back of the leaves. Spray these with an organic, contact insecticide. Sparrows may peck at the flowers, reducing crops. Grow white flower varieties which are less attractive to birds, or protect with netting big enough to allow bees in to pollinate flowers, but small enough to keep birds out! Pick beans young for tender flesh and best flavour.

> ### QUICK TIP
> **Dwarf runner bean 'Hestia' (Marshalls) makes short, bushy plants which can be grown in a pot 8in (20cm) across and 10in (25cm) deep filled with good potting or multipurpose compost.**

Step by step ▶ Growing perfect runner beans

1 Pick a sunny, sheltered position with deep soil. Dig in rotted manure in autumn, or make a trench, fill it with veg scraps and green waste, cover with soil.

2 Don't sow outside, in the soil, until late May. Sow 5 seeds per 6in (15cm) pots from mid April. Keep frost free (on a windowsill indoors). Plant out in May.

3 Put up a wigwam or sturdy double row of canes approx 12in (30cm) apart. Tie them securley. Set one plant per cane, or sow two seeds by each one.

4 Pinch out growing tips when plants reach the top of the canes. Water regularly. Pick beans regularly when they reach 8-10in (20-25cm) long.

Quick tips

July
...more things to do

① Making pot-pourri

■ MAKE POT-POURRI from dried flowers scented with essential oils. For a dry pot-pourri, harvest flowers as they begin to open. For colour use flowers such as golden rod, larkspur, marigold, pansy and globe amaranth. In the case of roses, go for the strongest colours.

② Checking tree ties

■ BY THIS TIME in the season, woody plants will have had a growth spurt, and their girths will have increased. It is important to check that the ties securing young trees to their stakes are not too tight; if they are, they'll constrict the flow of sap in the tree and it will suffer.

③ Removing rose suckers

■ SUCKERS SPROUTING from grafted rose rootstocks grow vigorously in summer. Keep them in check as they will quickly take over the top grafted cultivar, and the suckers are unlikely to flower. Remove them by snipping them off at the base.

④ Deadheading annuals

■ REMOVE THE faded flowers and/or flowerheads of all types of bedding plants. By promptly removing them you will be encouraging the plants to produce more blooms, and so extend the season of colour. Feed with a tomato fertiliser to help the plant make new flowers.

⑤ Collect ripe seeds

■ IF YOU WANT to raise summer-flowering plants from your own seed, start collecting now. If you delay too long the seeds may well drop into the garden soil. Safeguard those not quite ready to pick by placing a paper bag over the seed head, tied around the stem.

⑥ Protect yourself

■ YOU'LL BE SPENDING LONGER out in the garden now, not just to keep on top of all the jobs that need doing, but also to enjoy it. Remember to protect your skin against strong sunshine – especially your face, arms, shoulders, back and legs – with a suitable sunscreen.

AUGUST 2013

THURSDAY

1

FRIDAY

2

SATURDAY

3

SUNDAY

4

MONDAY

5

TUESDAY

6

WEDNESDAY

7

THURSDAY

8

How to grow spring cabbages

SPRING CABBAGES fill the 'hungry gap between the end of the winter vegetables in March, and early summer crops. They are easy to grow from seed. Sow seeds in late August to overwinter outdoors in the soil and harvest in spring. Sow seeds directly in the soil in a seed bed. Choose a sheltered, sunny site. If your soil is acidic, add garden lime a couple of weeks before sowing/planting

1 Rake the soil and water it well. Draw a short 'drill' or groove in the soil, 2ft (60cm) long and ½in (12mm) deep, mark each end with a stick and put in a label. Water the drill well.

2 Sow seeds about ½in (12mm) apart into the drill. Cover very lightly with soil, and cover the area with fine netting supported on hoops. Put down slug pellets, weed regularly. When plants reach 6in (15cm) tall, transplant into rows 18in (45cm) apart (pictured). Set plants up to the base of the bottom two leaves, 12in (30cm) apart. Water them in, scatter a few slug pellets then cover with netting or a cloche. Pigeons love cabbages! Weed around plants, keep slugs and snails at bay. Harvest plants from late winter.

AUGUST 2013

FRIDAY
9
SHREWSBURY
FLOWER SHOW

SATURDAY
10
SHREWSBURY
FLOWER SHOW

SUNDAY
11

MONDAY
12

TUESDAY
13

WEDNESDAY
14

THURSDAY
15
SOUTHPORT
FLOWER SHOW

FRIDAY
16
SOUTHPORT
FLOWER SHOW

Beat wasps

WASPS ARE BOTH good and bad in the garden. In the first half of the year they feed on insects such as aphids, helping to keep plant pests under control. Then around midsummer, they get a taste for sweet things, such as garden fruit like plums and apples – or our food when we're eating out. And wasps (below) sting. Don't confuse wasps with hoverflies, which look similar but they're smaller, they don't sting, and they are good for the garden.

To control wasps either use jam jars or cut off drinks bottles (above) or buy wasp traps. Fill them with sweet liquid such as sugar water, fruit juice or beer, and hang them in trees and bushes – away from where you're sitting! Empty traps regularly and refresh the sweet liquid. Have a fly swat handy for persistent little blighters.

If you have a lot of wasps there may be a nest nearby. Your local council can send a pest control specialist to dispose of the nest.

AUGUST 2013

SATURDAY
SOUTHPORT
FLOWER SHOW
17

SUNDAY
SOUTHPORT
FLOWER SHOW
18

MONDAY
19

TUESDAY
20

WEDNESDAY
21

THURSDAY
22

FRIDAY
23

SATURDAY
24

New strawberry plants for free

STRAWBERRIES propagate themselves by producing runners (stolons) from around June each year. If you're growing strawberries in the soil you can allow them to take root, to form what is known as matted rows alongside the parent plants. By doing this you'll get more strawberries, but they'll be smaller than if you'd cut off the runners. Runners sap the energy of the parent plant, so in general it's best to cut them off (right). The same goes for strawberries grown in containers or growing bags.

However to refresh your plants every three or four years, you can 'strike' a few runners and grow them on as new plants.

To do this, don't cut the runners off the parent plant. Make staples with little hoops of bent wire. Where rosettes of leaves form on the runners, peg these firmly onto the soil (or pots filled with John Innes

No 2 compost – pictured) and water well. Left for six to eight weeks like this the plants will take root. They can then be cut from the parent plant, and replanted in a fresh bed.

AUGUST 2013

SUNDAY

25

MONDAY

26

TUESDAY

27

WEDNESDAY

28

THURSDAY

29

FRIDAY

30

SATURDAY

31

Drying flowers

DRYING FLOWERS is a fun and creative job – the perfect home project for you to get kids involved in during the summer holidays. Dry flowers brighten up the house during the autumn and winter, providing long-lasting and maintenance-free floral displays. There are three ways to dry flowers, depending on how high their water content is, and what you want them for.

Drying flowers in a desiccant
■ Flowers with a high water content (big, soft petals and stems) such as iris don't air dry well – you'll need to dry them in a desiccant (dry sand, silica gel or cat litter). To do this line a sturdy box with your chosen desiccant about 1in (2.5cm) deep. Remove the leaves from the flowers, then place them face down into the box. Sift more desiccant over the flowers until they are completely covered. Place the lid on the box and store them in the airing cupboard. Leave to dry for two weeks.

Air drying flowers
■ Air dry flowers in small bunches (up to 10 stems - pictured) so that rots don't set in. Tie stems together carefully using twine, then hang the bunches in a warm, dry area like an airing cupboard, or shed in the summer. They should take three to four weeks to dry out.

Pressing flowers
■ Pressed flowers are great for making into pictures or greetings cards. All you need is a couple of heavy books and some absorbent paper. Place one piece of absorbent paper onto a flat surface, put the flower on top then place another piece of absorbent paper on top of the flower. Carefully place both books on top of the paper to flatten the flower, and leave for a couple of weeks.

Your gardening week

If you go on holiday...

10 steps to keeping garden plants happy when you're not around to tend them

MANY OF us will be taking a summer holiday over the next few weeks. But it won't just be us soaking up the sun – our garden and house plants will, too. Without water, plants in pots or in dry soil will die. Pests and diseases left untreated will quickly spread and you could return to a garden looking like it's been through World War III!

It doesn't have to be this way. If someone can cast a quick eye over the garden every three or four days, watering needs or pest and disease attack can be spotted and dealt with quickly.

The best idea is for a friendly neighbour to take over the watering while you're away (especially one who is a keen gardener) – in return letting them harvest any crops and flowers that are ready.

There are some people that offer a paid-for service, but it can be expensive. If these options aren't possible, you'll need a back-up plan. Here's one that will work:

2 Install automatic irrigation

■ A great way to keep your garden watered, with no supervision. It takes water from the tap via a timing device, through a system of drip irrigation hoses. Try the Hozelock Aquapod – prices start at under £20.

3 De-bloom and harvest

■ IF PLANTS are allowed to set seed they will have reached the end of their cycle and die back. To stop them doing this, be ruthless and pick all of your crops including immature fruits that may ripen while you're away. Also remove all spent, and open blooms on flowering plants, especially in pots and baskets.

1 Care for houseplants

■ DON'T FORGET about your houseplants! Place capillary matting (available from most garden centres) on to your draining board, trailing into a full sink. Let the matting soak up water then place your house plants on the matting, well spaced out.

4 Plants in pots

■ GROUP OUTDOOR pots together in a shady spot, which will slow growth and reduce water loss through transpiration. Standing them on trays filled with gravel and water will keep the atmosphere around them humid for a week or so. Do not feed plants just before you leave – rapid growth requires more water. Remove flowers.

5 Bottle irrigation

■ WATERING SPIKES attached to old, water filled drinks bottles are pushed into the compost around pot plants. The water drips from holes down the spike. A 1ltr bottle can last up to two weeks – less when it's hot. Thompson and Morgan (Tel 0844 2485383, www. thompson-morgan.com) sell this product.

8 Undercover crop care

■ TENDER CROPS, such as tomatoes, cucumbers, aubergines and chillies in a polytunnel or greenhouse, will need immediate attention. Give them a really good water and remove any scorched leaves or stems. Pick any crops that are ripe. The following day, give plants a high-potash feed, such as Tomorite.

6 Weed beds and borders

■ WEED THROUGH beds and borders, and around the tops of pots and containers, thoroughly. Weeds compete with garden plants for moisture.

9 Love your lawn

■ IF YOUR LAWN has turned brown, don't worry, as a few decent rainfalls, and it will soon get back on its feet. However, if the grass is very tall, cut it with the mower blades set at their highest, or use a strimmer. The following week, drop the mower blades to the next setting down. After that, cut as normal. Tidy edges with lawn shears.

Here's what to do when you get home:

7 Tackle containers first

■ GIVE ALL POTS a really good water. If the compost is very dry, plunge the pot into a bucket of water and leave it to soak for 30 minutes. Move all containers back into the sun and spread them out. A few hours later water pots again with liquid fertiliser added. If you've been away for a long time (two weeks or more) be prepared for some casualties.

10 And finally...

■ HARVEST RIPE crops and water everything. Check all plants for pests and diseases– either pick off pests or infected leaves, or spray with a suitable pesticide or fungicide. Weed through beds and borders, tie in to supports climbing or tall plants that may have flopped over, using twine or a cushioned wire. Now you can have a cup of tea!

Messing about on the river

Words and pictures Phillips/Hurst

We walk the plank to see how **Elaine Hughes** has decked out seven Thames barges with plants in the heart of London

Garden notes

Name: Elaine Hughes

Address: Downings Road Mooring Barge Gardens, 31 Mill Street, Southwark, London SE1 2AX

Size of garden: 25yd. x 4yd. (23m x 3.7m)

Special features: A series of unique floating gardens on the River Thames that have been planted on top of seven residential barges. Walkways connect the boats in dock with the shore. Each garden has an individual character and the planting includes vegetables and herbs as well as trees, shrubs, fruit trees, and herbaceous perennials

ELAINE HUGHES has one of the best gardening jobs you could imagine. Not only does she get fantastic views of London's iconic Tower Bridge but, even better, it allows her to work from home for three or four days a week in the summer.

Elaine lives on a boat moored on the River Thames at Southwark. And it's here that she has created and now maintains a unique medley of floating gardens on top of seven barges. The gardens act as walkways for up to a dozen boats at a time,

with the living accommodation tucked down below. Central pathways run along the top of each barge, lit in some places by strings of fairy lights. There is nothing like the Downings Road Moorings Barge Gardens anywhere else in London.

Unique opportunity

Created on the top of old Thames Lighters, and at 25yd. (23m) long x 4yd. (4m) wide, the garden presented Elaine with a unique opportunity. Although she is a landscape architect more used to designing public spaces, she has found her professional skills just as helpful here.

"I had to consider the depth

of soil available, as well as the aspect and climate," Elaine explains, "and think about how all these conditions would affect the plants. This is an exposed site with a specific climate – plants dry out very quickly here so I needed to pick things that would cope."

But there are some problems that are different from any other type of gardening.

"It's much harder to get access to the plants, and I've had to get used to crawling around the deck on all fours and hanging off the edges of the boats," she says.

Elaine finds the popular lilac flowered perennial Verbena bonariensis (below, in the foreground) a useful plant on the boats and it is one of many, including marigolds and poppies, that she allows to self-seed, giving the barges a common floral link

"I was absolutely terrified at first, especially when the tide was high and passing boats created a swell! I got used to it, but I'm still wary about going round the edge of the boat – there's quite a strong current."

Elaine grows vegetables for residents, there's an area for herbs and even a barge for social get-togethers.

"There's a real mix of people and a strong sense of community," says Elaine. "By doing the gardens I have got to know all the residents and we often meet up for a drink."

Waterproof deck

The gardens were first planted nine years ago. In order to provide a safe planting environment each one was fitted with a waterproof deck, drainage to prevent waterlogging and a membrane

> ## 66 There's a real mix of people and a strong sense of community 99

to keep the soil in place. Before planting began, 30 tons of good quality topsoil had to be lifted into the planting areas by crane from another barge.

Today there's a huge selection of plants, ranging from holly, apple and quince trees to herbaceous artemisia, marigolds, poppies and ornamental grasses.

"Each barge garden is quite different but there are plants common to all and I also let things self-seed as much as they like," Elaine explains.

"As we don't have deep soil here I go for shallow-

rooted plants such as *Robinia pseudoacacia*, ilex (holly) and even oak because it grows so slowly and so is easy to manage.

"But some plants, such as lavender, just don't seem to work so I'm still experimenting to see how well things grow and how quickly.

"All the plants are fed with organic plant food," Elaine says. "I try to encourage a natural eco-system whereby the bugs control themselves."

A wigwam of runner beans in flower looks ready to produce a good crop. Elaine aims to use colourful vegetables which are also attractive, either for their flowers or foliage. Asparagus, rhubarb and globe artichokes are among the veg she favours

Lighting along the central walkway helps guide residents returning to their boats at night. Despite the shallow soil, planting is dense, with cardoon thistles and nepeta providing ground cover, and trees such as birch and copper beech

> ## 66 I'm still experimenting to see how well things grow 99

Your gardening week

Ornamental garden

Deadhead your flowers

if you want them to keep blooming

IF YOU WANT a long lasting display from flowering plants in borders, pots and baskets, it is important to remove dead or fading flower heads before the plants set seed. Withering blooms should either be plucked (in the case of soft stemmed bedding plants) or snipped (from roses and other woody stemmed plants) just above a pair of leaves beneath the flower head.

Done promptly, and removing the whole of the flower head, you will prevent the plant setting seed.

Flowering is all about reproduction for plants, so when they've made seed to create the following generations, they'll stop. Annuals just fade away and die while shrubs and perennials will stop flowering until the following year.

Sweet peas

■ CLIMBING SWEET PEAS have very delicate blooms. It's worth picking the flowers as soon as they've opened and displaying them in a vase indoors. The flowers set seed and fade so quickly it's difficult to keep up. If you pick all of the flower stems that appear, you can enjoy the colour and scent indoors without worrying that the plants will go over quickly.

Roses

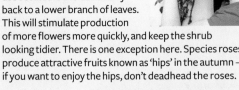

■ MANY GARDENERS just pull the fading flowers off the stems of roses. While this is better than leaving the flowers in place, you'll get a better result on repeat flowering roses if you use secateurs and cut cleanly back to a lower branch of leaves. This will stimulate production of more flowers more quickly, and keep the shrub looking tidier. There is one exception here. Species roses produce attractive fruits known as 'hips' in the autumn – if you want to enjoy the hips, don't deadhead the roses.

Foxgloves

■ FOXGLOVES and other plants that produce tall flower spikes, including lupins, delphiniums and verbascums, will all benefit from deadheading. You should wait until the main part of the flower stem has gone over then use secateurs to cut back to a side branch lower down the stem, or right down to the ground if there are no side branches apparent.

Bedding plants

■ ALL OTHER annuals and perennials growing in borders, pots and baskets will benefit from having dead blooms removed. It's a job that's worth concentrating on once a week – in a large garden it can take some time! If it has been left longer and the plants are looking a bit the worse for wear after deadheading, give them a liquid feed such as Miracle Gro (above) to boost new flower production.

The Classic Gardener

Peter Seabrook

Bulb size matters

The size of bulb you buy can affect the flower quality – **Peter** explains how

BIG IS BEAUTIFUL when it comes to most of the spring-flowering bulbs now on sale; the bigger the bulb, the larger the flower and/or numbers of flowers each one will produce.

While many of us might be tempted to buy on price, we are more likely to get value for money if we buy by bulb size. Take for example tulips, most of which are sold in prepacked bags and are 10-11cm/up in size (which refers to the bulbs' circumference).

While these will grow and flower well next spring, they are not the pick of the bulb crop. Search out at least 12cm/up or bigger in size if you want to plant good and deep and have them coming every year with no special treatment.

I have two beds of roses, one underplanted with May-flowering tulip 'Maureen' and the other more recently planted with Darwin Hybrid tulip 'Red Impression'. 'Maureen' must have been in my heavy soil for nearly twenty years, flowering freely every late April before the new rose foliage appears.

Both of these were originally bought in size 14cm/up, with the view to getting a long flowering life. It is logical that the largest bulbs selected from a crop are likely to last longest.

Daffodils and narcissus are a bit different in that they all naturalize pretty well and flower year after year until the clump becomes very dense. However,

> *"The largest bulbs from a crop are likely to be more vigorous"*

larger bulbs of any given cultivar will yield more flowers, so once again we get more for our money.

Choice of daffodil cultivar is very much a matter of taste. I wasn't sure about split-corona types at first, but having seen unusual pink and apricot bicolours artistically arranged in vases, the plant breeders' skills are better appreciated. Forced to make a choice, the golden trumpets of 'Dutch Master' and fragrance of 'Old Pheasant Eye' take some beating.

We should remember scent when choosing bulbs for spring, especially if they are grown to cut. Narcissus 'Fragrant Breeze', (white with apricot-yellow cup) is worthy of the name, having freesia-like scented flowers. Similarly, choose single early tulip 'Apricot Beauty' and tulip 'General de Wet' for fragrance. Grown in pots under cold glass, 'Apricot Beauty' is a lovely, paler apricot colour and makes a beautiful bloom for vases.

Top tips ➤ 3 bulbs well worth planting

Nacissus 'Faith' is eyecatching and sales of bulbs raise money for the charity Breast Cancer UK.

Narcissus 'Jetfire' with swept back perianth and contrasting orange red trumpet is a good cultivar.

With hyacinths smaller sized bulbs produce shorter flower spikes that stand up better to rough weather.

Gardener's tea break

SPOT THE DIFFERENCE

Summer – the perfect time to relax and enjoy the peace and quiet of the garden, as our cartoon clearly shows! But can you spot the four differences between the two cartoons? Answers are below.

(Answers can be found at the bottom of the page)

WORDSEARCH

```
E Y T N A L P G G E
P R M U L P I T V L
O R T I I N O O J K
R E O N G C L R O N
T B K E I I L R N I
O P R R V M E A Q W
I S P E S O R C U I
L A L M O N D T I R
E R E D N E V A L E
H C A E P X O L H P
```

This word search contains the official names of 17 colours, all of which are associated with plants or fruits. These words are listed below; in the grid they may be read across, backwards, up, down or diagonally. Letters may be shared between words. Erroneous or duplicate words may appear in the grid, but there is only one correct solution. After the listed names are found there are 6 letters remaining; arrange these to make the **KEYWORD**.

ALMOND	JONQUIL	PHLOX
APRICOT	LAVENDER	PINK
CARROT	MINT	PLUM
EGGPLANT	OLIVE	RASPBERRY
GINGER	PEACH	ROSE
HELIOTROPE	PERIWINKLE	

IT'S RECYCLING TIME!

Mailbag

MY PARTNER is an horologist (clockmaker) and he recently chucked out some old clocks. I thought this one was quite attractive so I drilled out the centre of the dial, fitted a plastic meat tray inside to hold moisture, and planted Petunia 'Million Bells'. It certainly brings a smile to our customers' faces as they come to the workshop.

Mr J Jozkow, Holyhead, Gwynedd

Problem solver

Q Mrs S Woolset from Great Yarmouth, Norfolk, writes: I have been given two beautiful hydrangeas, one white and one blue. Could you please tell me how I can ensure they do not change colour?

A The colour of hydrangea flowers is influenced by the pH (acidity) of the soil in which they are planted. On alkaline soils that contain lots of chalk, blue hydrangeas will tend to flower pink. On acid soils, pink hydrangeas will tend to flower blue.

So to keep your hydrangea blue, aluminium must be present in the soil. This can be added by applying aluminium sulphate at 4oz per sq yd (136g per sq m) around the plant. White hydrangeas cannot be altered, though as they age they have a pinkish tinge to the petals.

Quick tips

August
...more things to do

① Water cuttings

■ TAKE EASY 'water cuttings' of tender perennials such as petunias, verbena and coleus (pic). Cut 4-6in (10-15cm) long young shoots and place them in jars or small vases of water on a bright windowsill. Roots will soon form and plants can be potted up into John Innes No2 compost.

② Stop butterflies

■ ENSURE BRASSICAS on the veg plot are netted to stop cabbage white butterfly, and check daily for eggs on leaves. Caught in time they can be rubbed off before they hatch into caterpillars. Netting mesh size should be 7mm.

③ Shading plants

■ MOVE POTS and baskets to shadier areas if going on holiday to help reduce water loss. Grouping your pots together will also make the task of watering easier for your neighbour. This will help ensure that no pot is forgotten.

④ Soak spring shrubs

■ CAMELLIAS, RHODODENDRONS and other spring flowering shrubs will be starting to develop buds for the next flowering season, so keep them well watered, regularly. Dryness at this stage can cause buds to drop off before they open and flower.

⑤ Remove suckers

■ Remove competing suckers (growths appearing around the base) from trees and shrubs, especially those growing on grafted forms, in pots or in the garden beds. Remove suckers by pulling at their base rather than cutting, so they are less likely to come back.

⑥ Improve greenhouse light

■ SHADING FROM greenhouses an now be taken down, and/or greenhouse glass paint removed. Clean the glass to make sure light levels are used to their full potential as the days get shorter.

⑦ Protect ponds

■ NET PONDS and large water features before autumn leaf fall begins. Ensure the netting is fitted securely to avoid damaging the plants. Net size should be big enough to let wildlife escape.

SEPTEMBER 2013

SUNDAY

1

MONDAY

2

TUESDAY

3

WEDNESDAY

4

THURSDAY

5

FRIDAY

6

SATURDAY

7

SUNDAY

8

Refresh lawns

THERE'S NOTHING nicer than walking on, running on, rolling on or just sitting on a fresh, green lawn. But all of these things take their toll. The soil becomes compacted so grass roots get no air, and rain water puddles on the surface, effectively drowning the little grass plants.

To stop this happening, take a good solid garden fork, drive it 6in (15cm) deep into the turf, waggle it around (picture 1), and repeat at 6in (15cm) intervals across the entire lawn! Yes, it's a monster job, but it will let your grass breath again. For an even better result, after spiking the area, top-dress with ½in (12mm) of John Innes No3 compost (picture 2) and brush or rake it across the lawn so it falls down the spike holes you've made.

TOP TIP
Between now and mid October you can apply an autumn lawn feed to strengthen root growth for winter. Do not use a summer lawn feed.

SEPTEMBER 2013

MONDAY

9

TUESDAY

10

WEDNESDAY

11

THURSDAY

12

FRIDAY

13

SATURDAY

14

SUNDAY

15

MONDAY

16

Roses for free!

Take hardwood cuttings of your favourite roses

MOST ROSES, with the exception of hybrid tea types, can be propagated from hardwood cuttings taken in September and October after flowering – just when you should be pruning, which is perfect. Cuttings taken now will be ready for planting out, where you want to grow them, in a year's time.

Step by step — Hardwood cuttings

1 Dig a slim, 5in (12.5cm) deep trench in a sheltered spot, long enough to take your cuttings spaced 4in (10cm) apart. Fill the base of the trench with horticultural sand or 'sharp' sand.

2 Take 12in (30cm) long cuttings from the base of healthy stems (at least 3 buds on each cutting). Cut just above a bud at the top, just below a bud at the base. Remove all foliage.

3 Push the base of each cutting into the sand with buds facing up, spaced 4in (10cm) apart. Backfill trench with soil, firming around each cutting. Water well, label with variety.

SEPTEMBER 2013

TUESDAY

17

WEDNESDAY

18

THURSDAY

19

FRIDAY

20

SATURDAY

21

SUNDAY

22

MONDAY

23

TUESDAY

24

Xmas hyacinths
Festive season flowers

FORCING SCENTED hyacinths to flower at Christmas is quite easy – it's all about timing. You must buy special 'prepared' bulbs or they won't flower in time. In mid to late September, set your bulbs in a pot (with drain hole) filled with bulb fibre or any good, open compost. The top of each bulb should be just poking out of the compost (pictured). If you put several bulbs in one pot, they can be close but should not touch each other or the pot sides.

Water and allow to drain. Put the pot in a black plastic bag, and stand it in a cool, dark place like the shed.

Check regularly. When new shoots on the bulbs are 2in (5cm) tall bring them indoors to a cool, dull room. When the leaves green up, move them to a bright position which is a little warmer (but away from radiators). Water when the compost gets dry.

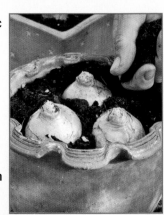

SEPTEMBER 2013

WEDNESDAY

25

THURSDAY

26

FRIDAY

27

SATURDAY   MALVERN AUTUMN SHOW

28

SUNDAY   MALVERN AUTUMN SHOW

29

MONDAY

30

Picking apples

THERE'S A SIMPLE secret to picking apples and pears when they are completely ripe. Cup your hand under each fruit and gently lift and twist (picture 1). If the fruit comes away from the branch easily without pulling, it's ripe. If it doesn't, leave it and try again a few days later.

When the fruit on each tree ripens will vary depending on variety, but the lift and twist technique will ensure you don't harvest too early.

Tall fruit trees can be quite a problem – lifting and twisting is out of the question! However a fruit picker on a long arm, such as the Darlac Fruit Picking Basket (picture 2) will make life a lot easier.

Some varieties of apples, and cooking pears, will store for up to three months.

Ornamental garden

Your gardening week

Seasonal bulb colour

Garden centre shelves will be full with autumn and spring bulbs you can plant now

P LANTING BULBS is an easy way to bring colour to the garden in autumn and next spring. Bulbs are available from garden centre and DIY stores now, you just have to plant them and wait for their colour to burst forth.

There's no need for frost protection – crocuses are renowned for blooming even when covered in a layer of early spring (best planted in November to avoid the risk of tulip fire disease), spring flowering bulbs should be in the ground no later than the end of September.

You can plan your bulb displays for one big hit of colour – simply choose varieties which flower at the same time – or choose a mix of varieties that will give you a prolonged show of colour from February through to May (such as snowdrops, crocus, iris reticulata,

daffodils and muscari).

There is also still time to plant autumn flowering bulbs, such as Colchicum 'Water Lily' and 'The Giant'.

Planting bulbs is a simple task. For a regimented look space bulbs out evenly on the surface before planting. Alternatively, you can throw them in the air (not too high!) and plant them where they land for a more natural look.

QUICK TIP
Get out to buy your chosen bulbs as early as possible – popular varieties sell out quickly

Three ways to plant bulbs in the garden this autumn

1 Beds and borders

■ DIG OUT THE AREA you want to plant, deep enough for the bulbs plus an inch of grit in the base. Space bulbs over the grit cover with a soil, firm in and water.

Planting depth

■ AS A GENERAL RULE, planting depth is determined by the size of your chosen bulbs. Take the length of the bulb and plant it 2-3 times deeper than the measurement. So, if your bulbs are 2in (5cm) long, plant them 4-6in (10-15cm) deep in the ground.

2 Individual bulbs

■ USE A BULB PLANTER to dig individual holes in the lawn, deep enough to add some gritty compost to the base. Drop in your bulb and backfill, placing the turf patch back on top.

Multiple bulbs in grass

3

■ USE A HALF MOON to cut a 'door' into the lawn. Lift three sides of the turf with a spade, dig out soil to reach the planting depth. Set bulbs, cover with the lifted soil and firm back the turf.

Planting bulbs in pots and containers

■ PLANTING SPRING bulbs in pots means you can move the colour to where you need it – on the patio, between plants in the borders to fill gaps, or on a windowsill outdoors. Once planted they can be pretty much forgotten about until they break through the surface in February to May – just don't let them dry out. Even then, winter weather should take care of watering.

Only use frost-proof pots. Your containers will be exposed to everything our winters can throw at them, and freezing conditions will shatter poor quality terracotta. No bulb likes sitting in wet conditions, so provide good drainage with grit in the bottom of the pot then use free-draining specialist bulb compost to fill it. Finish with a layer of grit or gravel mulch for a smart look.

QUICK TIP
Spacing in pots can be relaxed, but aim for 2in (5cm) of compost below bulbs and at least 1/2in (1.2cm) in between bulbs

Step by step ▶ Plant a pot of spring bulbs

1 Add a good inch or two of grit to the bottom of your frost resistant pot for good drainage.

2 Add at least 2in (5cm) of bulb compost, firm down, and set out your bulbs. Put plenty in!

3 Cover with the required depth of compost, gently firm and level, then cover with grit and water in.

Care over the winter

■ POSITION POTS out of weather and temperature extremes, a sheltered shady spot or cold frame is ideal

■ During extreme cold, place in a frost- free location such as an unheated garage, greenhouse or shed

■ IF THIS isn't possible wrap individual pots in plastic bubble wrap

■ Cover pots with wire mesh to stop squirrels, mice and voles digging up bulbs, but remove it as growth appears

■ AS SPRING approaches, place the pots in a sunnier position to get them growing

Plant in layers

■ WHEN WORKING with a mix of bulbs in one container, plant them in layers. Set taller growing, larger bulbs that need the deepest planting first. Cover with compost and then add a layer of smaller bulbs. Avoid positioning bulbs directly on top of each other.

Autumn razzle-dazzle

Plantswoman **Annie Bullen** selects some of her favourite perennials and shrubs for late colour

Lobelia tupa – this dramatic autumn perennial is in the same family as the ordinary blue hanging basket lobelia

Hardy plumbago (Ceratostigma plumbaginoides) has brilliant blue flowers and foliage that turns a rich orangey-red in autumn. It teams up brilliantly with roses – try 'The Fairy', which will keep on flowering from June through to September

WELL, YOU'VE folded away those beach towels, shaken the sand from your shoes – and tutted over the weedy, overgrown state of your far from colourful garden. But don't despair, it takes just a few hours to tidy up and deliver an injection of flower-power that will bring your garden back to life.

The trick is to look for plants that bloom prolifically as the days shorten – and to keep deadheading those that flower until the first frosts.

For sheer colour you can't beat some of the shrubby salvias in bright blues, stunning scarlets, purple-blacks to die for, clear yellows, pure whites – and the most shocking of pinks. The hardier types such as *Salvia microphylla* will be fine over the winter as long as they're given a sunny spot and well-drained soil. Grow the tender types, like *S. elegans* and *S. involucrata* in large pots and take them undercover over winter, or take cuttings to overwinter in the greenhouse.

You can't go wrong with dahlias, as long as you regularly deadhead. When I lived in mild Cornwall, my neighbour took pride in cutting dahlias right up to Christmas. The orange varieties, such as 'David Howard', 'Catherine Deneuve', and

'Kenora Sunset', will team well with the strong blues of your salvias, as will the near-black flowers of the dahlia 'Arabian Night'. Deep shocking pinks such as dahlias 'Fascination' or 'Excentrique' also tone in with strong blues and maroon shades.

ANNIE'S AUTUMN STARS

■ ASTERS ARE a great glory of the autumn. Fill your garden with glowing pinks, reds, plums, purples and rich violets and blues of these Michaelmas daisies – and watch the warmth come back. Try the dramatic *Aster lateriflorus* 'Lady in Black' with dark leaves and clouds of pale flowers, or the smaller dark-leaved 'Prince', to add a touch of class.

■ YOU MIGHT not believe it but some roses can flower well into the autumn. 'The Fairy' (pictured left) is a fantastic polyantha rose with great clusters of small double pale pink flowers, and makes a good shrub 3-4ft. (1-1.5m) high. It will produces colour non-stop from late June until December. Its slightly lax habit means that it combines well with other plants.

■ ROSES TEAM up well with hardy plumbago (*Ceratostigma willmottianum*) which will thrive in a sheltered border and give great pleasure for the intense blue of its long-lasting flowers and lovely rusty autumn leaf colouring.

■ FOR A finishing touch – it's not easy to grow – but what could be more thrilling than the devil's tobacco, the 6ft (1.8m) tall *Lobelia tupa* from Chile, with its clusters of twisted brick-red flowers and soft felted light green leaves? It needs plenty of moisture in summer, and protection from wet and extreme cold in winter. This giant quirky lobelia will reward you with a fantastic show from July to the end of October.

SHORT ON SPACE?

■ IF YOU'VE NOT got any room left in the borders for autumn colour, or only have a tiny plot to garden on, why not consider creating a special container to give a flash of autumn colour? Any of the following plants will give an eye-catching show

ASTER DUMOSUS (PICTURED)
DAHLIAS (GO FOR SHORTER FORMS)
HEUCHERA (VARIOUS)
JAPANESE ACER
NERINE BOWDENII
ORNAMENTAL GRASSES
AUTUMN/WINTER PANSIES
PHYSALIS ALKEKENGI (CHINESE LANTERN)
SEDUMS (VARIOUS)

SUPPLIERS

■ **Van Meuwen**
℃ 0844 557 1850
www.vanmeuwen.com

■ **Hardy's Cottage Garden Plants**
℃ 01256 896533
www.hardys-plants.co.uk

Ornamental garden

Your gardening week

Making compost

Making compost can save the expense of buying soil conditioners and mulches

HOMEMADE COMPOST takes time to break down and mature into something usable, but it's a brilliant way to recycle garden waste, turning it into a soil conditioner which will save you money and improve your garden.

The type of compost bin, and what you fill it with, both affect how quickly green waste rots down. A big bin, once full, will process waste more efficiently than a small bin because it gets hotter. Care should be taken with ingredients.

QUICK TIP

Regularly turn the compost heap to allow in air and speed up the process

You need to add a balance of soft green (leafy) material, and woody waste such as plant stems or newspaper. For quick results it's best to chop up or shred it all, and mix it thoroughly.

If you have room, tip the contents of the bin out after six weeks, then pile it back in. This mixes the ingredients and adds air, which will speed up decomposition. The addition of products such as compost activator Garotta may also help. Very dry composting material should be watered a little after adding it to the bin.

The composting process can take from four to 12 months. It's ready when it's crumbly and dark brown, with little or no smell.

Here are some ideas on how to start a bin:

What can I compost?

DO add:

■ LAWN CLIPPINGS, hay/straw, raw kitchen peelings, tea bags, egg shells, leaves, non-seeded weeds, wood chips, sawdust, vegetarian pet droppings

DON'T add:

■ COOKED KITCHEN waste, meat, bones (all attract rats), carnivorous pet waste, diseased plants, pernicious weeds like bindweed and knotweed (weeds and diseases can survive the composting process)

Step by step ▶ Filling a standard garden compost bin

1 Stand the bin on bare earth, and add a 4in (10cm) layer of fresh material – grass cuttings, chopped up plant material, raw kitchen peelings, tea bags, eggshells, newspaper and other waste that will rot

2 Apply a sprinkling of J. Arthur Bower's Garotta (2-3 tablespoons per square metre/yard) as a compost activator to speed things up, or instead you could use a little granulated balanced fertiliser, or stable manure

3 Water the fresh composting material until fully wet. Repeat these steps over the coming weeks until the bin is full, leave it for six weeks, give it a thorough turning with a fork, and leave for a further 3-4 months

Step by step > Make a large pallet composter

1 Clear away plant material and other debris and level the site. You may need to fork over the soil, rake away any excess and then firm to ensure the pallets stand on stable ground and line up properly.

2 Place the first pallet at the back of the area, on edge. Slide two tree posts through the top of the pallet and hammer them in with a heavy mallet. Aim to drive the stakes a good 12in (30cm) into the ground.

3 Place the two side pallets at right angles to the back pallet. Butt them up together and ensure everything is square before fixing the side pallets in place with tree stakes, as in step 2.

4 To strengthen the construction, tie the pallets together with sturdy wire. Use two lengths on each of the corners and twist tight with pliers. Repeat this on the two end stakes to hold side pallets in place.

5 Cover the inside of the pallets with mypex membrane to retain heat in the compost, speeding up the rotting process. Use a hammer and galvanised flat-headed nails, or a staple gun, to fix in place.

6 For access, create a door by placing a final pallet across the open side. Fix with wire top and bottom on one side to create 'hinges'. Or wire both sides lightly so pallet can be removed easily for access.

Step by step > Make a dustbin composter

1 Use a 1in (2.5cm) paddle drill bit to make holes in the sides and bottom of a plastic dustbin. These can be randomly placed but I've opted for spaced rows on the sides, with 3in (7.5cm) between holes.

2 Pull away plastic shavings. Upturn the bin and stand it on four bricks. This aids aeration and improves ventilation – but stand it somewhere that won't matter when compost liquor leaks from the bin.

3 Aim to fill your bin quickly for a fast turnaround. After each 4in (10cm) of material, apply 2 tbsp of compost activator. When full, wet the material and close the lid. Leave for 12-14 weeks to break down.

Composting on a small scale

■ IF YOU WANT TO COMPOST all your kitchen waste, you could invest in a Bokashi bin. This is a container with airtight lid and integral tap, plus a supply of Bokashi bran inoculated with micro-organisms that can compost kitchen waste in just a few weeks.

Every time you have scraps to throw out, be it meat, fish or vegetable, drop them in the Bokashi bin along with a sprinkling of the bran and re-seal the lid. When the bin is full, leave for two weeks and then dig the resultant compost into the garden, or add it to your larger compost heap. The Bokashi bin produces a nutrient-rich liquor that can be drawn off via the tap. Diluted with water it makes great plant food.

Reliable plum crop

Bob has a sneaky way of making sure he has an annual supply of plums

Plums are a marvellous addition to the fruit cage, but the trees will grow too large to contain in time

THERE ARE some well-known problems with plums – not in the growing, as the trees are fairly easy and trouble-free. No, the problem is with their habit of fruit production.

You see they can crop sporadically, sometimes only once in three years or more. But then they do so with a huge glut. For example, in some places the frosts catch the blossoms or young fruits year after year after year.

Then you get lucky – they miss the frosts, and the trees crop in such profusion they really do break their own branches (so prop them before they do so, and lighten the load – shears will do the job).

With these trees in 'on years' you often get so many plums you don't know what to do with them. And they've no sale value, as everyone else around you also has loads.

Of course almost every one has 'Victoria' (pictured), and there's nothing wrong with that. It's a good, dual-purpose plum.

But there are many other good ones you could plant, such as 'Pershore' (a tart yellow type for jamming), and the even more 'jammable' variety 'Purple Pershore'. 'Marjoree's Seedling' is also a popular choice, as is 'Csar'.

But along with plums there are the gages, so similar but with a sharper, more aromatic, flavour. 'Oullins

"Coe's Golden Drop could be mistaken for a type of apricot"

Golden Gage' and 'Golden Transparent' rival mangoes, though admittedly they are a tad smaller! And the divine (but needing a warm spot) 'Coe's Golden Drop' variety, which could be mistaken for an apricot.

But there is another problem with plums. They don't stay small. They need space. The old-fashioned rootstocks just did not dwarf them, though more recent ones look promising. Plums I've grown in containers proved thirsty, light croppers and were rather short-lived.

However I do believe I've come up with a scheme. As I said, they crop sporadically, but then in such glut you'll gladly give them away. So I'm buying a range of choice varieties as presents for friends and neighbours. Thus I'll get as much variety of fruit as I want in the years they do crop!

Do it now Topical tips for organic gardeners

Pot up plants of mint with rootballs as big as possible, for forcing under cover through autumn

Place slug traps in amongst stored potato crops to keep the damage they cause to a minimum

Prick the ground with a fork before oversowing bald patches in the lawn with grass seed

Gardener's tea break

CROSSWORD...
just for fun Answers below

ACROSS
1 The common name for coleus (or solenostemon) is _____ nettle (5)
3 Type of troublesome mildew disease (5)
7 The white head of a cauliflower (4)
8 To get down close, to do some weeding, one usually has to get down on at least one ____! (4)
9 An era, found in the herbs borage and lovage! (3)
11 The pot marigold genus (9)
14 '___ Alf Ramsay' is a type of dahlia, and '___ Anthony Hopkins' is a type of *Calluna vulgaris*! (3)
16 Tissue surrounding the seed in certain fruits (4)
17 Sounds like a fertilised ovule, containing an embryonic plant, but it really is to give in! (4)
18 Genus of the mountain 9 down (5)
19 Broom made from a bundle of twigs tied onto a shaft (5)

DOWN
1 The 6 down genus (5)
2 Common name for the agapanthus (7,4)
4 Common name given to certain plants of the anemone family (11)
5 The harvest, and even what it weighs perhaps (5)
6 Fruit from a semi-tender, exotic-looking tree, of the 1 down genus! (3)
9 Geum is generally accepted as the _____ genus, but 18 across is the genus of the mountain type! (5)
10 Small tree of the sambucus genus, having white flowers in a cluster, followed by purple berries (5)
12 Leafy vegetable, often the suffix to ruby or Swiss – akin to spinach (5)
13 Dairy-based *Calluna vulgaris* 'Spring _____' (5)
15 Sedum is frequently referred to as the ___ plant (3)

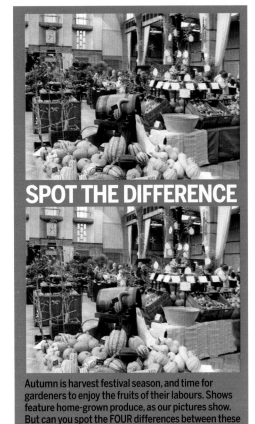

SPOT THE DIFFERENCE

Autumn is harvest festival season, and time for gardeners to enjoy the fruits of their labours. Shows feature home-grown produce, as our pictures show. But can you spot the FOUR differences between these two images? (Answers can be found at the bottom of the page)

YOU RANG?!
This sign was the last thing I wanted to come across in the garden centre – my wife doesn't need any encouragement!
Mr Giblin, Penarth, Vale of Glamorgan

Mailbag

SALVIA
Hot Lips

YOUR HUSBAND RANG – IT'S OK TO BUY AS MANY PLANTS AS YOU WANT!

Problem solver

Q Mr Muir from Harrogate, North Yorkshire, writes: Last year I bought a passion flower that was doing really well on a south west-facing wall. But when the flower buds were ready to open the plant shrivelled and died. What I am doing wrong?"

A It is probable that the plant dried due to extreme heat and dryness at the roots. The south west-facing wall may be too hot. If you plant another, add compost when planting, and water well when the buds are bursting. Additionally, feed with sulphate of potash monthly from April to August. Mulch to insulate roots against high temperatures.

CROSSWORD ANSWERS ACROSS 1 Flame 3 Downy 7 Curd 8 Knee 9 Age 11 Calendula 14 Sir 16 Aril 17 Cede 18 Dryas 19 Besom **DOWN** 1 Ficus 2 African lily 4 Windflowers 5 Yield 6 Fig 9 Avens 10 Elder 12 Chard 13 Cream 15 Ice

SPOT THE DIFFERENCE The central barrel is missing a band and the tip of a squash (centre) has changed from yellow to red. Another squash (centre) has lost its green stripes, and a hessian cloth (right) has changed colour.

Your gardening week

How to grow
strawberries

Britain's favourite fruit is surprisingly easy

THE SUCCULENT acid-sweetness, vibrant colour and acute seasonality of strawberries have all contributed to their popularity – though seasonality is now only an issue for gardeners.

The most common garden-grown types are short-cropping 'summer' strawberries, but 'perpetual' types which crop right through summer are available. The fruits are high in fibre, and packed with Vitamin C, manganese and flavonoids.

Varieties to try

'Finesse' (from D. T. Brown)
Perpetual cropper with great flavour

'Christine' (from Suttons Seeds)
Very early fruiting summer type

'Alice' (from T&M)
Mid-season summer type, sweet and juicy

SIMPLE STEPS TO GROWING SUCCESS

SITE & SOIL
■ CHOOSE A sunny, sheltered site with rich, moist, free-draining soil. Improve with well-rotted manure or garden compost in winter. Add a dressing of balanced fertiliser before planting. If you're growing in containers they should be large and deep with drainage holes, and filled with a good quality potting or multipurpose compost.

WHEN TO PLANT
■ PUT IN new, bare-root plants from June to September in the soil outdoors. Potted plants can be started in the greenhouse in pots and beds in early spring, but are best established in autumn to fruit the following spring.

PLANT IN THE SOIL
■ TO PLANT bare root strawberries, dig a shallow trench, mound the soil in the base to create a ridge down the centre, set bare roots 18in (45cm) apart, spreading the roots out over the ridge. Cover with soil so the crowns are ½in (1cm) below the surface, firm in and water well. Set pot-grown plants 18in (45cm) apart, but at the same level as they are growing in their pots. Space rows 24in (60cm) apart.

IN CONTAINERS
■ USE BIG, deep pots (pic 1) – if putting in more than one plant space them 12in (30cm) apart. Position in full sun. Use multipurpose compost. Water in well.

ROUTINE CARE
■ WATER PLANTS regularly. Give a high potash (tomato) feed from mid-spring, fortnightly until fruiting declines. Mulch soil-grown plants with straw (pic 2) to rest developing fruits on. Allow container-grown fruits to dangle above the ground. Pick off slugs and snails. Remove mouldy fruits and bin them. Use netting to protect ripening fruits from birds. Remove runners (long, thin stems) unless you plan to strike new plants from them.

HARVEST
■ PICK FRUITS as soon as they reach an even, deep red colour all over.

Smartideas

Strawberry 'runners' – long stems with baby plants at the end – can be pegged to a pot of moist, gritty compost and when rooted, cut away from the parent to grow into new stock plants.

Quick tips

September ...more things to do

1 Hanging baskets

■ KEEP BASKETS going through September by feeding and dead heading. Rainfall can be varied from now on so check the dryness of the compost and water regularly. Check for signs of disease and remove all infected material.

2 Planting for spring

■ START TO PLANT out any spring-flowering biennials like foxgloves and wallflowers (pictured with tulips), in their final planting positions. If they have been grown under cover, harden off first by moving outdoors by day and back in at night for up to two weeks.

3 Clean and sharpen tools

■ CLEAN TOOLS, especially secateurs, ahead of autumn pruning so they don't rust or harbour diseases. Use an oily rag to clean blades, removing and sharpening if badly blunted. Then oil working parts.

4 Clear up windfall fruit

■ START TO GATHER up and bin or burn bad fruit that has dropped from trees. This will help to stop diseases spreading. Leave a few in a pile, in a corner of the garden for the wildlife to enjoy.

6 Rambling roses

■ RENOVATION OF rambling roses can start now. Cut some of the old woody branches to the ground, keeping six young stems to tie to supports. Remove all dead, diseases and damaged stems first and saw away any dead stumps to stop disease entering the plant.

5 Order stock for winter planting

■ IF YOU ARE THINKING of putting in bare root plants such as roses or trees, start to look now. Nurseries sell out of certain varieties quickly, especially if on dwarfing rootstocks. Research varieties now, well before you need them.

OCTOBER 2013

TUESDAY

1

WEDNESDAY

2

THURSDAY

3

FRIDAY

4

SATURDAY

5

SUNDAY

6

MONDAY

7

TUESDAY

8

Autumn gold

THE LEAVES of many deciduous trees in Britain turn a glorious colour before falling to the ground. It's a joy that's often followed by a lot of grumbling from gardeners as crinkled brown leaves swamp flower beds and lawns, or choke ponds. They must be raked up or they can seriously damage plants and lawns by blocking out light, or rot in water causing ponds to go stagnant.

But the leaves of deciduous trees make a wonderful soil conditioner if they are collected, stored in a bin or a plastic bag and left to decompose.

The leaves of trees are rotted by fungus rather than bacteria (which makes garden compost decompose). They should be raked up, packed into loose wire cages made of chicken wire, and kept moist. Alternatively wet them thoroughly, pack them tightly into plastic bags with a few holes punched in the sides, tie the top and tuck them somewhere out of sight. In a year or two's time the leaves will have broken down into wonderfully light, crumbly material that can be used as soil conditioner.

OCTOBER 2013

WEDNESDAY

9

THURSDAY

10

FRIDAY

11

SATURDAY

12

SUNDAY

13

MONDAY

14

TUESDAY

15

WEDNESDAY

16

Prepare ponds for winter

THERE ARE a couple of important jobs to do now if you have a pond or water feature in the garden. First, cut back fading and dead pond plant stems and leaves – use secateurs as some can be quite tough.

Remove all of them and put them in the compost bin. Now roll your sleeves up, and lift out dead leaves and debris from the water – go deep down and collect as much of the sludge and debris off the bottom of the pond as you can reach. All of this material can rot, making the water stagnant.

Don't worry about stirring up silt – it will settle again in a few days. Leave debris on the side of the pond for a day to let aquatic creatures escape back into the water, then compost it. Finally, fix a net just above the surface of the pond. It

should have a mesh small enough to catch autumn leaves and stop them from falling into the water. You can lift and divide pond plants at this time of year if they need it, or wait until spring.

OCTOBER 2013

THURSDAY

17

FRIDAY

18

SATURDAY

19

SUNDAY

20

MONDAY

21

TUESDAY

22

WEDNESDAY

23

THURSDAY

24

Warming your greenhouse

IN MOST parts of the UK gardeners will need to install some kind of heating to keep the inside of greenhouses frost-free through winter. This is important if you overwinter tender plants in the greenhouse, or raise early seedlings in spring.

All Greenhouse heaters have a maximum area they can maintain at a set temperature. Before buying your heater, measure the dimensions of your greenhouse and choose a model to suit its size.

QUICK TIP
Fixing bubble wrap against the inside of all greenhouse glass will greatly reduce winter heating costs

■ Paraffin heaters and bottled gas

Paraffin or gas powered heaters are portable, cheap and the carbon dioxide gas given off can benefit plants. However, careful ventilation is needed to reduce any build up of fumes and water vapour. High humidity will promote fungal diseases. The heaters will need checking regularly and refilling with fuel. However you don't need a qualified professional to install it as you do with electricity. Light the heater whenever frost is forecast. Always store paraffin and gas safely out of the reach of children.

■ Electric fan heaters

Convenient, cheap and easy to control, electric heaters produce no water vapour. Available from most garden centres, they have a thermostatic switch and turn on automatically when the temperature drops below a preset level, so they require little attention once plugged in. By law, wiring mains electricity to your greenhouse must be done by a 'Part P' qualified electrician. Check local authority listings for tradesmen.

OCTOBER 2013

FRIDAY

25

SATURDAY

26

SUNDAY

27

MONDAY

28

TUESDAY

29

WEDNESDAY

30

THURSDAY

31

Plant perennials

NOW IS a good time to plant a range of perennials that will give you colour and interest throughout the following year. You might try hellebores for spring, alstroemeria for summer and Acanthus spinosus (known as bear's breeches) for autumn colour. Space plants carefully depending on how big they will grow. Fill gaps between plants with spring and summer bulbs.

QUICK TIP
Label perennials after planting, especially if they die back, so you can remember where they are in your bed for next season

Step by step Planting hardy perennials

1 Water the plant well if in a container. Bare root perennials supplied by nurseries need to soak in a bucket of water for an hour or two. Dig a hole twice the size of the rootball.

2 Add a little fertiliser to the planting hole. Knock the pot off the plant and check for signs of pest and disease on roots; tease roots out gently if they are congested.

3 Pop the plant in the hole so top of pot compost is level with the top of the planting hole. Backfill with soil, firm gently around the roots, then water in thoroughly. Label the plant.

Your gardening week

Plant trees & shrubs

Get plants in while the soil is still warm

AUTUMN IS a great time to plant all types of trees and shrubs, as well as woody climbers. These plants create form and structure in a garden – they are often described as the 'backbone' of planting – so it's important to choose carefully, plant them properly, then help them to establish well.

Before you buy, there are a few key considerations. First anticipate the eventual height and spread of your desired plant and make sure it will fit the space. Then look at soil requirements including acidity – does yours measure up? Does the plant need sun or shade; will it survive if your plot is exposed to strong winds; and will it thrive in the temperatures in your locality – half hardy plants are always at risk.

Buying tips:

■ Choose plants with green, healthy leaves (except in winter when deciduous plants lose their leaves) and no stems dying back. Also check for pests or diseases.

■ **With evergreens, ensure stems are well clothed with leaves.**

■ Is the plant symmetrical in shape, and has it been well-maintained, with no leggy stems?

■ **Check the roots by lifting it out of the pot (above); the rootball should hold its shape without compost falling off, but it should not be clogged with roots.**

Buying tips:

■ Soil collapsing from the rootball when raised from the pot suggests that the plant has recently been lifted from the open ground and potted up – don't buy it.

■ **Dense surface weed growth (pictured), along with dry soil and/or large, exposed roots coming from the base of the container, shows that the plant has been poorly maintained.**

■ Pots with splits or tears should be avoided.

What size to buy?

■ Don't just buy the biggest tree or shrub you can afford. Larger (and older) specimens are costly and take a long time to settle in – they may even be overtaken by younger, more vigorous and cheaper specimens. However smaller plants, although cheaper, will probably take longer to reach a good size when planted.

Stepbystep Planting a tree or shrub

1 Once you've chosen a site for your new tree or shrub, dig a generously sized hole. It should be twice as wide and deep as the plant rootball.

2 Pile the spoil beside the planting hole. Use a fork to break up the soil in the base – this is especially important if the soil is heavy clay.

3 Hammer in a stout stake at one side of the hole to support the new plant, and add well rotted manure or compost to the planting hole.

4 Take the tree or shrub out of its pot. Now carefully loosen and tease out some of the roots from the sides and bottom of the rootball.

5 When siting the new plant in its hole make sure it is sitting at the correct level, with the top surface of the rootball level with the surrounding soil.

6 Backfill around the rootball with the displaced soil, and firm it in place with your feet; it's crucial to press out any air pockets around the roots.

7 Watering in the tree or shrub is very important. This is done to settle the soil closely around the roots, so really soak the soil, several times.

8 Once planted, it can be useful to look over the plant and remove excessively long branches, or to cut away unbalanced shoots.

New ways to plant

■ The latest thinking on how best to plant a new tree or shrub is to dig a hole just deep enough to take the rootball but a fair bit wider than it needs to be, then fork over the bottom of the hole.

Experts now say you should not add manure or fertiliser to the planting area as this is believed to inhibit natural growth of the root system. Not adding plant food forces the roots to go looking for nutrients and moisture, which in the long term will give you a healthier tree. However they do recommend adding mycorrhizal fungus (such as Rootgrow) to the soil when planting; this helps roots to take up nutrients.

Autumn vs spring planting

■ Container-grown plants can be planted in the garden at any time of year, but 'bare root' plants from specialist nurseries should only be planted in autumn or winter.

■ Evergreen trees, shrubs and conifers are best planted from early September to mid-October, while the soil is still warm. If you miss this slot, then choose April, when the winter chill will have left the soil.

■ Deciduous woody plants should go in from mid-October to mid-April, ideally November to March when they are fully dormant. Avoid planting if soil is frozen, or very wet.

A former presenter of BBC2 Gardeners' World, Alys is known for her thrifty gardening advice

Spring into action

The bright, crisp mornings of autumn are perfect to get you in the mood for a spot of bulb planting, says **Alys Fowler**

I CAN'T HELP but feel excited by autumn. There's something about that shift in light, the first cold evenings and those brilliant, bright mornings. It comes just as I start to long for woolly jumpers and toasted teacakes.

For the gardener, autumn is about bulbs and all that they can bring to the following year. There are too few bulbs in my garden – some ill thought-out large daffodils, some hastily planted muscari and just six pink tulips. Next spring will be different as I intend to splurge on a huge amount of small bulbs. A few years ago, the German supermarket Lidl had great sacks of bulbs for pennies. Most were hideously garish types of tulips and overly large frilly daffs, but there were gems to be found.

> *"Autumn is about bulbs and all they bring to the following year"*

I spotted 'Rip Van Winkle,' a shaggy miniature daffodil, the pale white form of *Crocus vernus* and several stripey ones, plus *Narcissus* 'Tete-a-Tete'.

So this year I will venture back to the supermarket to see what's on offer. The rest will come from garden centres and mail order. The trick is to get there early as the plumpest bulbs go first!

My grape hyacinths (muscari) thrived, despite being plonked in quickly

Shallow planting

Of all the spring bulbs, you can leave the tulip and daffodil planting to last if you're pushed for time. Neither seem particularly bothered by a late arrival. If the daffs fail to flower next spring, they'll sort themselves out by the following year.

If you're planting tulips for temporary bedding then

I scour garden centres, supermarkets and mail-order suppliers to source good deals for my garden

it's possible to put them in just 2in. (5cm) or so underground. Unless they have very heavy blooms they won't mind shallow conditions and it does make pulling them out at the end so much easier.

Another simple trick is to grow your tulips in pots and plunge them around the garden where necessary.

But I prefer to stick with a few choice tulip species that can remain in the ground; all that digging up, storing and replanting drives me crazy!

Last but not least, I want every one of my currants to be surrounded by a halo of blue and pink in spring. I'm going to combine the vigorous *Chionodoxa* 'Pink Giant' with *Scilla bithynica*. Fingers crossed!

Alys's tips

1 The autumn-flowering *Colchicum speciosum* can be naturalised in grass under fruit trees and in orchards where mowing regimes can be relaxed.

2 Old Pheasant's Eye narcissus and fritillaries are an arresting site in long grass. They need damp conditions to thrive and spread.

3 Other bulbs for naturalising include *Anemone nemorosa* and its many cultivars. They're ideal in damp litter – conditions often found under deciduous trees.

Kitchen garden

Your gardening week

How to grow
garlic

Try this rewarding crop that stores well

IT'S EASY to grow good garlic in British gardens. Plant the cloves in autumn, around late October, giving roots plenty of time to grow over the winter so plants get away strongly in early spring. The plants need colder temperatures (lower than 10°C) for a couple of months to initiate the formation of cloves.

You can plant in spring, but they won't do as well in a poor summer. Another option is to plant garlic into large pots filled with JI No3.

There are around 30 varieties of garlic available, and two main types. Softnecks are the ones normally available in the shops and the bulbs tend to be larger and store well. They don't produce a flower spike. Hardneck varieties include some real gourmet types, such as 'Red Sicilian', with spicy flavours and amazing colour. These produce a flower spike that needs to be cut off to allow the bulb to continue to increase in size (you can eat the flower spike!). Bulbs for planting are available from garden centres in the autumn, or mail order from specialist growers like The Garlic Farm.

Step by step — Follow this easy guide for a great crop of garlic bulbs

1 Break a bulb of 'seed' garlic (from garden centres) into individual cloves. Dib holes 4-6in (10-15cm) deep and 8in (20cm) apart, rows 12in (30cm) apart, in well prepared soil. Drop one clove, pointy end up, into each hole. Cover with soil.

2 Before the end of the year, green shoots will appear. Sprinkle granular fertiliser such as growmore around plants in spring. Keep weed-free, water as necessary. Cut off flower spikes that appear in late spring. Harvest when leaf tips go yellow and fade.

3 Lift autumn planted bulbs with a fork from end of May to July. Spring-planted bulbs are harvested from midsummer to early autumn. Lay bulbs out to dry. To store, trim off dry roots and either plait in ropes like onions, or cut off the dry stem and store in netting sacks.

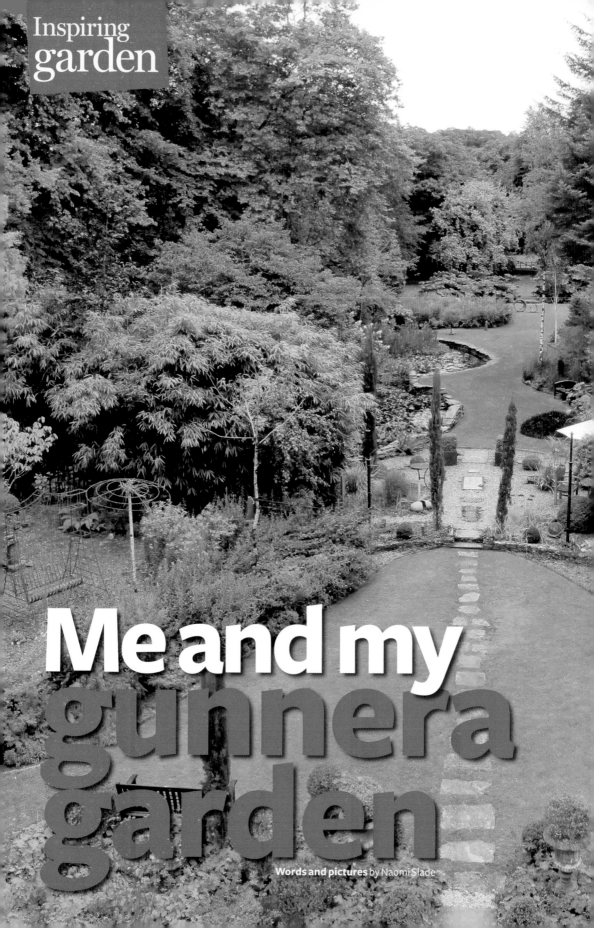

Me and my
gunnera
garden

Words and pictures by Naomi Slade

It may not be quite as scary as the fictional sci-fi triffid plant but Gunnera manicata, with its spiny leaves and funky flower spikes, can reach huge proportions.

Garden notes

Name: Nick Priestland

Address: The Cors, Newbridge Road, Laugharne, Carmarthenshire

Size of garden: About an acre (with more land to cultivate)

Soil type: Boggy, acidic, mainly peat

Aspect: South

Special features: Dramatically planted garden encircled by water and including ponds and a large bog garden. Planting is adapted for the wet ground and includes many spectacular gunnera. The artist owner has made his mark with all sorts of creations including a wire 'shade umbrella' and seat in a pond.

Season visited: Summer

Structural plants add fascinating detail in a garden. Here, the veins of giant gunnera leaves form dramatic patterns. Cannas, bananas and even edibles, such as courgettes, can be used in a similar way.

Nick Priestland has used gunnera and other water-loving plants to overcome a high water table and boggy site. Modern art and structural contrasts complete the look

Use an unusual specimen tree to create an impact on the lawn. Here a baby swamp cypress, Taxodium distichum grows. Known as the 'bald cypress', because of its winter leaf loss, it thrives in damp ground.

NICK PRIESTLAND'S atmospheric and artistic garden in a wooded valley, near the Taf estuary in South Wales, is a lasting testament to his determination. The long vista is pinched in at the middle to form a screen, and opens out beyond. There are no frilly herbaceous borders and primary colour roses here, rather a confection of big planting with a minimalist and masculine colour scheme.

But this is a garden with a unique challenge – water. The River Coren forms the right hand boundary and splits just upstream, effectively turning the plot into an island. With pools and springs in the middle, it's no wonder that the property name

Nick's background as an artist is clear in the way he uses patterns and objects in the garden. The middle of this old sign for his restaurant rotted and fell out, creating an instant frame for some three-dimensional plant art.

– The Cors – means 'bog' in the Welsh language.

"When we arrived 20 years ago it was totally wild," says Nick. "There were brambles and *Rhododendron ponticum* everywhere! It had never been treated as a garden before. It was more like a flooded paddock!"

But Nick, an artist and restaurateur, rose to the challenge magnificently. Clearing the ground, he used the springs to form ponds. "Believe it or not all these ponds had to be dug by hand. The ground is so wet the machinery sank!"

He has embraced water-tolerant plants in all their forms and

Use herbaceous perennials like geraniums with exotic specimens. Nick has also planted Ligularia dentata 'Desdemona' with irises and jagged-leaved Melianthus major with soft grasses.

A prehistoric boggy wilderness evokes a time when dinosaurs roamed the land. Grasses, pines, gunnera and the towering stumps of tree ferns are a great starting point.

Nick's taste for symmetry can be seen in the repeated shapes of mounds, cubes and spheres, while the upright pickerel weed in the pond echoes cypresses by the house.

the result is striking. Bamboo thickets and wild planting have an almost prehistoric feel. Glossy, healthy stands of pickerel weed, (pontederia), erupt from the pond and there is a thriving population of *Gunnera manicata* and its smaller relative *G. tinctoria*.

"Size matters!" says Nick. "The garden is big enough to take it and gunnera suits the situation, soil and dampness very well. I keep splitting them up and moving them around. They are very architectural and adaptable." He propagates his gunnera by splitting up the rhizomes with a spade. "You get a big chunk and it only takes a year or two to catch up with the main plants," he adds.

The palette of green emphasizes contrasts of texture and leaf form, and Nick has added to this shades of copper and bronze in the form of acers, cercis and *Cotinus coggygria*. "Being a painter I wanted it to have a 'painterly' feel," Nick explains. As a horticultural canvas it seems he has got the brush strokes just about right!

Your gardening week

Dividing perennials

Lift and divide established border perennials to improve vigour and give you more plants

1

P LANTS IN a well-tended herbaceous perennial border should ideally be divided and replanted every three years to keep them vigorous and contain their size. Late September and October is the best time to tackle this job.

If you tend a large planting area it is best to split the plot into three so that a third of the plants are divided each year.

It's amazing how rough you can be when dividing perennials but there are of course some sound principles to follow for success.

Firstly, lift the whole plant, keeping as much of the rootball intact as possible. Many plants can be split by inserting two garden forks in the centre of

QUICK TIP
Before replanting divisions of perennials back into the border, improve the soil with garden compost or well rotted manure, and a couple of handfuls of bonemeal to boost root growth over the winter.

the rootball, back-to-back (picture 1) and using them to lever the rootball in to two or more sections (picture 2). Plants with dense, hard roots such as bamboo are best divided using a spade blade or saw (picture 3), while smaller plants with looser root systems can be teased apart by hand.

Replant a good, vigorous piece in the border display after improving the soil with compost, and pot up spare divisions individually in a multipurpose compost and soil mix (picture 4).

2

3

4

Top tips for dividing perennials:

- Divide summer flowering perennials in autumn or spring

- **Divide spring flowering varieties in summer after flowering**

- Shake off excess soil from rootballs before dividing so you can see what you're doing

- **For fine or dense roots the rootballs can be washed in a bucket of water to reveal the root system more clearly**

- Keep new divisions well watered for successful re-establishment

- **Keep potted divisions in frost-free conditions over winter. Replant in spring once soil temperatures start to warm up**

- After thinning your display by division, set out slug and snail controls as these will be the main pest threat during establishment

Dividing oriental poppies

■ PERENNIAL ORIENTAL POPPIES (*Papaver orientale*) are grown in many gardens, and they really thrive if regularly divided. They're easy to tackle – so a good plant to learn on if you're new to dividing perennials. The individual plants within the clump are easy to identify and come apart without too much difficulty. Here's how to go about it:

Step by step

1 Water around the roots of the plant you plan to divide and leave it for an hour or so. When you return, dig up the whole of the plant ensuring as much of the root ball as possible comes with it.

2 Either pull the clump of plants apart with your hands, keeping some root on each piece, or ease them apart with a fork or spade. You can be quite rough – you may need to be! Bin any divisions showing signs of disease.

3 Remove outer leaves to divert energy into root growth. Replant a vigorous division into the border soil after digging in a bit of garden compost or well rotted manure. Firm in with your heel. Water in really thoroughly.

4 Pot up some of the spare divisions to give to friends or plant out elsewhere in the garden. Plant them firmly in pots of John Innes No 3 compost, water in well and stand them in a bright, sheltered spot.

Dividing delicate perennials

■ SOME PERENNIAL PLANTS have very delicate stems and root systems, such as primulas (right) and succulent sempervivums (left). These can usually be lifted easily with a hand fork, then teased gently apart with fingers, replanting individual rosettes or small groups of rosettes. Also take care with tuberous perennials like dahlias – carefully wash soil off the tubers, select individual swollen roots each with a bud at the top, and cut off close to the crown of the plant.

Gardener's tea break

WORDSEARCH

A	E	P	S	P	O	H	T	I	L
I	T	C	A	R	B	A	A	T	A
R	T	S	I	I	E	I	N	C	L
E	E	H	U	H	T	E	C	A	U
V	S	P	G	N	L	U	P	C	S
E	F	H	U	U	Y	Y	B	L	S
H	F	P	C	Y	O	L	Y	E	A
C	O	C	U	M	A	R	R	O	R
E	U	T	R	E	S	E	D	L	C
S	B	I	R	L	E	R	R	A	B

This word search contains words, associated with cacti and succulents. These words are listed below; in the grid they may be read across, backwards, up, down or diagonally. Letters may be shared between words. Erroneous words may appear in the grid, and at least one word appears twice. But there is only one correct solution. After listed names are found there are ten letters remaining; arrange these to make the **KEYWORD**.

ALOE	DRY	REBUTIA
BARREL	ECHEVERIA	RIBS
BRACT	HEAT	SUCCULENT
CACTI	LITHOPS	SUN
CRASSULA	OFFSET	YUCCA
DESERT	OPUNTIA	
DROUGHT	PUYA	

ROOMS TO LET

I'VE MADE an insect hotel from reclaimed timber and it sits on a shelf in the courtyard where I live, firmly fixed to a wall. Unfortunately, I hadn't made it in time to attract any solitary bees so I hope that next year some of them will be taking up residence. The bottom section is made from a solid block of wood with holes of various sizes drilled into it. The middle section contains garden canes and the top part is filled with leaves, twigs, a section from an egg box and other bits and pieces. I've put up a Hotel Vacancies sign and I'm now waiting to see what happens!

Peter Little, Northallerton, North Yorks

Problem solver

Q Joan Jenvey emails: "What do I do with delphiniums and lupins over winter? Should I cut them down and cover them with straw? Even in late autumn they often still have leaves, and the delphinium sometimes blooms a second time."

A Both delphiniums (pictured) and lupins are hardy perennials, though both are short-lived and may only survive a few years. Delphiniums can have two flushes of flowers. Cut both plants down after flowering and cover with straw – or a mulch of grit if in heavy soil. This will keep them happy until spring when new growth will arise from the crowns.

SPOT THE DIFFERENCE

Every year, gardeners across the UK compete to grow the finest fruit and vegetables to win prizes at Royal Horticultural Society shows. Any crops that don't measure up will be swiftly rejected! But can you spot the **FOUR** differences between these two pictures? (Answers below)

Quick tips

October ... more things to do

1 Lawnmower care

■ BEFORE PUTTING mowers into storage for the winter, check blades and repair or replace if needed. Clean the machine thoroughly, and oil moving parts. If thinking of buying a new machine, look now as they are usually cheaper than in the spring.

2 Soil preparation

■ IF YOU have spare beds in the veg plot, or patches of soil in the herbaceous border, turn them over now to expose the soil to the first frosts. This will help reduce diseases, and the frost will also help improve the soil structure and expose weed seeds before planting next year.

3 Christmas cheer

■ AMARYLLIS (HIPPEASTRUM) bulbs, can be planted now for a winter display. They also make wonderful Christmas gifts to take around to neighbours and friends. Plant in 5in (13cm) pot.

4 Re-using plant labels

■ WASH OLD plant labels and, if plastic, remove pen marks with nail polish remover; they can be stored and used again next year. Washing labels also prevents any diseases on them from spreading.

5 Frost-free fleecing

■ DEPENDING ON the region in which you live, you may have to start thinking about fleecing outside salad crops from frosts. Horticultural fleece material is easily found in garden centres. Peg down, or attach to hoops.

6 Protect alpines from winter wet

■ CLEAR UP dead plant debris, and cover plants that may struggle in wet winter weather. Most alpine plants will cope with winter cold but in nature they actually remain rather dry under a winter carpet of snow.

7 Potting on

■ POT ON ANY SUMMER early summer cuttings that have taken well, showing root growth through the base and healthy top growth. If planting into the ground, the soil is still warm enough to encourage roots to take. And if potting into a pot one size larger, there is still time for the plants to settle before temperatures fall.

NOVEMBER 2013

FRIDAY

1

SATURDAY

2

SUNDAY

3

MONDAY

4

TUESDAY

5

WEDNESDAY

6

THURSDAY

7

FRIDAY

8

Storing crops

THE SECRET OF STORING fresh fruit and vegetables is to keep them dry, cool, dark and frost-free. They also need to be out of reach of mice and other pests. Apples and pears can be placed in trays with good ventilation, and stored in a dark corner of a shed, up off the floor.

Brush potatoes free of soil, put them in hessian or paper sacks and store in a cool, dry, airy and dark place.

Twist greenery off carrots (below) and beetroot, brush clean of soil and bury them in sand or dry compost in a box.

Dry onions (above) and garlic then store in nets, or their dried foliage (still attached to the bulb) can be twisted into ropes and the bulbs hung in a dry, airy spot.

Check stores regularly and remove any that are rotting.

NOVEMBER 2013

SATURDAY

9

SUNDAY

10

MONDAY

11

TUESDAY

12

WEDNESDAY

13

THURSDAY

14

FRIDAY

15

SATURDAY

16

A winter home for
friendly bugs

CREEPY CRAWLIES play an essential role in maintaining our ecosystem. They pollinate plants, aerate the soil, eat pests or provide food for other wildlife.

Bees, butterflies, hoverflies and moths are amazing pollinators, helping plants to make fruit and seeds. Ladybirds and lacewings eat aphids like greenfly. Violet ground beetles and their larvae prey on slugs and snails; and woodlice, worms and millipedes aerate the soil and break down organic matter.

Secure future generations by helping these bugs survive the colder months, and giving them a place to breed. Do this by placing suitable 'bug hotels' around the garden. These include simple piles of logs or stones, left undisturbed, which offer nooks and crannies for bugs to hibernate in. alternatively, you can make one out of a plant pot and some corrugated cardboard. Here's how:

Step by step ▸ Bug hotel

1 Thread string through the base then out of the front of a plastic flower pot. Now stuff newspaper in the base. Tie together up to a dozen 5in (12cm) long bits of bamboo cane

2 Wrap the canes in a piece of corrugated cardboard. Push this into the pot, and secure it by stuffing more paper tightly in between the card and the pot sides

3 Find a sheltered spot (wall, shed, tree or fence) for your 'bug hotel' and then hang it up on its side to prevent it filling with rain or snow. Then, just leave it for bugs to set up home in its nooks and crannies

NOVEMBER 2013

SUNDAY

17

MONDAY

18

TUESDAY

19

WEDNESDAY

20

THURSDAY

21

FRIDAY

22

SATURDAY

23

SUNDAY

24

How to make an onion rope

It works with garlic, too

CUT A 4ft (1.2m) length of strong twine or string, and tie the ends tightly together to make a big loop. Holding the knotted end, pull the loop to make a double length of string. Take a well dried onion – foliage still attached – and thread the neck through the loop, draw the foliage around the string and back through the loop. Support the onion while selecting another. Thread the neck of the second through the loop from the opposite side, draw its foliage around the string and back through the loop again. Keep adding onions like this, one side then the other, The weight of the bulbs will lock the ones below. Don't add too many if the bulbs are large – 8 to 10 will be plenty, but if bulbs are small you can add lots. Loop the foliage of the last bulb through the string three times to lock it, hang the 'rope' on a strong hook, and cut off the trailing bits of dry foliage.

NOVEMBER 2013

MONDAY
25

TUESDAY
26

WEDNESDAY
27

THURSDAY
28

FRIDAY
29

SATURDAY
30

Feed the birds

BIRDS ARE AN IMPORTANT part of the wildlife in our gardens, but they have a tough time through winter. Even when it's not snowing, the insects that birds feed on will be hibernating, and seed heads and fruits of garden and wild flowering plants are soon eaten up.

We can help by providing a regular supply of kitchen scraps, or proprietary bird food available from pet stores, supermarkets and garden centres. Food scraps include bread, bacon rind, dried and fresh fruit.

Packeted bird foods come in many forms. Some attract particular species. For instance Niger seed (which needs a special small-holed feeder) attracts goldfinches. Peanuts are great for tits. Mixed seed feeds keep robins, sparrows, blackbirds, starlings and other species happy. Fatballs will also prove very popular.

The most attractive seed to birds (and the most expensive to buy) is husked sunflower seed. Most birds enjoy this high-energy food.

Your gardening week

Pruning deciduous
trees and shrubs

Take care what you cut in the autumn

AUTUMN IS OFTEN TREATED by less well informed gardeners as the time to hack everything back for a jolly good tidy-up before winter sets in. However autumn is not a good time to prune many trees and shrubs. It is better to wait until late winter or early spring to prune a lot of woody plants, and some have particular requirements.

Cherries (prunus) for instance, are vulnerable to silver leaf disease if pruned in the autumn and winter – they should be tackled in early summer after flowering. Evergreens are usually tackled in early spring or after flowering; other (especially winter and spring flowering) species are best pruned immediately after flowering, while others still are best not pruned at all!

It may seem a bit of a minefield, but good gardening reference books published by the RHS will tell you the best time to prune specific garden plants, or you can look them up on-line. And remember, not all plants need pruning every year.

But there are some plants that should be pruned in the autumn, if they need pruning. Trees including beech, hawthorn and hazel (often used in hedges) are good candidates, as are acers. Climbing and shrub roses should be pruned in late autumn.

Vigorous growers like buddleja (pictured above), dogwoods (cornus) and lavatera can be reduced by half to lessen problems of wind rock over winter, then hard pruned in the spring to a new shoot low down the main stem(s). Shrub roses can also be treated in this way. Tie in stems of climbing roses then cut off any side shoots to three buds from the main stems.

The most important aspect of autumn pruning is removing dead, diseased or misplaced branches such as those that are crossing or rubbing against each other. Depending on the thickness of the stems to be removed, use either good, sharp secateurs; powerful loppers; or a pruning saw on thick branches.

Always aim to make a clean cut, either back to a bud on living wood with a pale green heart, or back to the stem it's growing from.

When using a pruning saw, first cut beneath the branch a little way away from the final pruning point, then cut from the top about an inch in front of the lower cut. Once the branch has fallen away, finish the pruning by removing the stump (left) with a clean cut close to the bud or point of growth.

After pruning scatter a few handfuls of bonemeal around the root area of shrubs to stimulate root growth over winter, and mulch with garden compost.

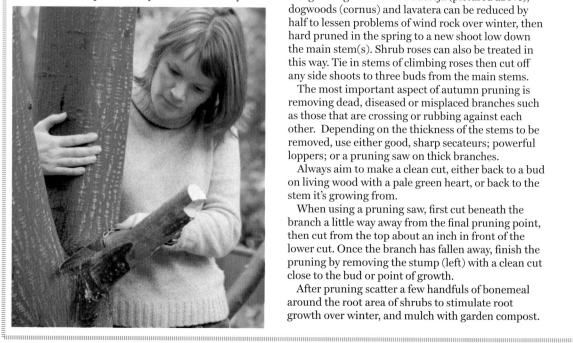

Moving deciduous shrubs and trees

■ LATE AUTUMN IS A GREAT time to move established deciduous shrubs and trees. It's heavy work, but worthwhile. Buying larger shrubs and trees is very expensive – moving one from its existing position to a new growing site just costs a bit of effort.

Plants up to about 8ft (2.7m) should be within the scope of most gardeners – any larger and you might need to call in the professionals.

Prepare the new planting site first so you can replant quickly, provide a support stake if necessary, and water the moved plant thoroughly once it's in.

Here's how to go about it:

Step by step > Moving a shrub or young tree

1 Dig a trench around the rootball, distance from the trunk should be about a third of the height of the plant - bigger if you can handle it.

2 Cut through thicker roots. Once you're down about 18in (45cm) start to undercut the rootball deeply, chopping with a spade.

3 Once the shrub comes free, drag the rootball onto sacking or mypex sheet and wrap the sheeting around it, tying it around the trunk.

4 Slide the plant onto a tarpaulin and carry it to its new planting site between two people. Unwrap the rootball and replant. Water well.

The showy pink blooms of Prunus 'Autumnalis Rosea' will flower on and off from November to March

Cherry **picking**

Not many trees flower during the winter months, which is why *Prunus* x *subhirtella* 'Autumnalis' is such a welcome treat. **Graham Clarke** explains how to grow it

W E'RE all familiar with spring-flowering cherries. They really go for broke with their big bunches of blowsy blooms, which can easily smother a tree. Even when these drop, the spectacular confetti-like clouds they create is legendary – often the subject of operas and poems.

But I prefer their lesser-known winter-flowering cousin, *Prunus* x *subhirtella* 'Autumnalis', for its steady supply of beautiful blossom at this chilly time of year. 'Autumnalis' actually refers to the start of its flower display, just as the peachy-orange colour from its autumn foliage comes to a close.

Although its flowers are more understated than those of its flouncier spring cousins, they continue on and off during the mild periods of the winter right through to March. When everything else in the garden is in a deep slumber, its flowers provide an unforgettable spectacle.

The *Prunus* x *subhirtella* species is Japanese, and most of its offspring are spring-flowerers: 'Autumnalis' and 'Autumnalis Rosea' are the only two winter-bloomers – the latter has flowers that are more markedly pink.

'Autumnalis' is a broad, spreading, deciduous tree; even when clothed with its small green leaves, it does not cast a lot of shade. It's capable of reaching a height of 27ft (8m) at maturity, but often reaches much less, making it suitable therefore for all but the smallest of gardens.

The blooms are a delicate pink in bud, opening to white; they are semi-double, pendulous, and about

½in (1cm) across. As they fade they acquire pink tones again.

You can cut the branches for gorgeous displays indoors, too. If stems are cut just as the buds are bursting, then kept in water in a light spot, and not in an overly-heated room, they should look great for a good couple of weeks.

As well as flowering for almost half the year, winter flowering cherries offer excellent autumn colour. Just before the new flower buds break – around October-time – its leaves go from green to yellow, peach, orange and then coppery-red before falling. They're gorgeous!

BUYING A TREE

■ WHEN CHOOSING YOUR tree from a garden centre or nursery, try to get one that is 'bottom-worked' (you may find it labelled as a 'feathered maiden'). This means that it is grafted low down, 6-12in (15-30cm) up from the ground. These trees flower young, and allow you the chance to shape them as they grow.

Before the tree bursts into blossom, it gives a beautiful display of autumn colour

Prunus mume 'Beni chidori' is another winter flowerer that is more compact than autumnalis, so is better for small gardens or containers

HOW TO GROW

SITE

■ Choose a sunny site that is not too exposed, or windy. Planting in front of dark evergreens will help to show up the airy, pale-coloured flowers. Like all forms of prunus, this is a surface-rooting tree, which can be a disadvantage if you plant it in the lawn.

SOIL

■ Average loam – ideally enriched with garden compost and well-rotted manure.

HARDINESS:

■ Though very hardy, it is still a good idea to give shelter from cold winter winds.

PRUNING:

■ It should not need much pruning, only to keep it within bounds. Carry this out on a dry day in summer in order to reduce the risk of silver leaf and bacterial canker. Remove any dead, damaged or diseased wood as soon as seen.

PESTS AND DISEASES

■ Aphids and caterpillars can cause problems; bullfinches eat flower buds. Generally disease-free.

SUPPLIERS

■ **Ornamental Trees**
☎ 01257 265232
🖰 www.ornamental-trees.co.uk

■ **Bluebell Nursery**
☎ (01530) 413700
🖰 www.bluebellnursery.com

Ornamental garden

Your gardening week

Planting tulip bulbs

TULIPS OFFER a wide colour range compared to other spring flowering plants, and grow to heights from 6in (15cm) up to 30in (75cm). This gives scope to use them in different situations, from alpine displays to formal spring borders, tree and shrub underplanting and containers. By choosing a mix of early and late varieties it is also possible to provide flashes of colour that will last from late March through to June.

Tulip bulbs generally become available alongside daffs, crocus and the like, from September onwards. But you should hold off planting tulips until November to reduce the risk of tulip fire disease.

Planting in open ground

◼ TULIPS PREFER a sandy soil that is well-drained – they don't do so well in heavy soils. If working with clay soils improve the area before planting by adding sand, grit and compost to improve drainage. If you are planting in clumps or drifts dig a large planting hole, position multiple bulbs at the bottom and then draw soil back over them. If adding bulbs between spring bedding plants such as primroses and pansies, dig individual holes for each bulb. Plant the bulbs at least three times as deep as the bulb is long. Some of the taller late varieties can be planted as much as 9in (22.5cm) deep. Always have the pointed end facing up (below right).

Tulip fire disease

◼ SIGNS TO look out for are distorted and withered leaves, which may be covered in brownish flecks and a light fuzzy grey mould. Bulbs may rot and the flowers may fail to open, or be very small with spots on the petals. Infected plants are best destroyed. If you experience the problem, don't plant bulbs in the same spot for at least three years.

Stepbystep > Planting tulips in containers

1 Fill the bottom of your chosen (winter proof) pot with a layer of crocks for good drainage.

2 Add a layer of bulb compost so bulbs will sit at their required depth, then space bulbs over the bottom.

3 Once bulbs are set (pointed end up), cover with compost and carefully firm the compost down.

4 Retain moisture and reduce weed establishment by covering the surface with gravel, then water well.

Kitchen garden

Your gardening week

How to grow
broad beans

Easy to grow and highly productive plants

BROAD BEANS, also know as 'fava' beans, are a cool weather crop. Varieties can be sown in autumn and early spring to give a succession of pods to pick from early to mid summer. Plants are highly productive when well grown, and the beans can be eaten fresh from the pod and lightly boiled, or stored in the freezer.

Broad beans like a deep, rich, moist but free draining soil and plenty of sunlight. Some varieties can grow to around 3ft (90cm) tall and will need supporting to give the best crops. If you garden on a windy site, it may be better to grow a dwarf variety such as 'The Sutton' which only grows 10-12in (25-30cm) tall and generally doesn't need staking.

Harvest the pods before the beans grow huge. Small

beans about the size of a thumbnail, popped from the pod are sweet and delicious. As they get bigger the flesh becomes floury and the beans develop a thick skin. This can be removed by blanching the beans in boiling water then slitting the edge and popping the dark green heart out of the skin, before cooking.

SIMPLE STEPS

PREPARE SITE
■ CHOOSE A sheltered, sunny site with deep soil. Dig in garden compost or well rotted manure to improve its structure. In early November rake the growing site level, mark a row with a garden line and sow a hardy variety like 'Aquadulce Claudia'

SOW SEEDS
■ PUSH EACH large seed into the soil (picture 1) about 2in (5cm) deep, spacing them 8in (20cm) apart in the row. Rows should be 12in (30cm) apart. Two rows each about 8ft (2.4m) long will provide a heavy crop. Sow more rows each fortnight from February – providing the soil is not frozen or covered

in snow – to the end of April. Seeds can be sown in pots (picture 2) if the weather is very cold outdoors, and grown on to plant out at the above spacing in spring.

AFTERCARE
■ WHEN SEEDS germinate, cover the young shoots with fleece if the weather is harsh. If you are growing a taller variety, provide support. Push canes into the soil along the outside edge of each row, and tie string (picture 3) around them at 12in (30cm) and 24in (60cm) height. Water in dry spells. Pinch out the growing tips (the top 3in/7cm) of each plant when the pods at the bottom of the plant begin to fill out. If black aphids attack

the plants spray them with a contact organic insecticide such as soft soap. Pick pods (picture 4) when well rounded.

Charles Dowding is an organic veg expert and award-winning author

The Veg Gardener

Charles Dowding

Make no-dig veg beds

Charles Dowding explains how easy it is to start a new veg bed without digging the soil

N OW IS a good time to start a new veg bed on any weedy or grassy area, without digging. I have just made a new bed using a wooden frame that was already assembled, and simply filled it with a mixture of compost and well-rotted manure, without digging or preparing the soil underneath. It can be used immediately, providing the season and weather are favourable for sowing or planting.

I have made lots of beds like this with excellent results. Most of the plants' roots are initially exploring the bed's ingredients in the top six inches. Then after about three months the grass and weeds underneath have decomposed and provide even more nutrients for the growing vegetables above.

When filling beds with compost and manure, tread the organic matter down. You won't compact it because organic matter does not squash together in the same way as soil can, and plants like firm soil

Raised beds like this can be planted up as soon as they're made, and can be productive throughout the year

TOP TIP
If you don't have any home made compost, set up a bin now, and start composting all of your garden waste.

to make contact with and anchor their roots.

Now, in the winter, is a good time to set up a new bed. Deep frosts will soften lumps of manure and compost which are spread on top of the undug soil. Then in spring all you have to do is 'de-clodd' it in any dry spells. You just run a rake through, or tap it with a manure fork to break up larger pieces, and move towards having a lovely soft tilth for sowing and planting as the weather improves.

1

Make a simple frame with pressure treated timber, site it on grass or soil and fill with garden compost/rotted manure

2

Tread the filled bed down to expel air pockets. This will improve, not harm the structure of the growing medium

To make large beds like this, scatter compost on the grass and cover with cardboard weighted down with stones

Making large beds, no frame

You can make a raised bed frame the size you want, or buy one of the proprietary frames in plastic or wood available from specialist suppliers.

However another way is to forget the frame, and simply spread the weedy/grassy area you wish to cultivate with well rotted organic matter. If you don't have any, you can take the next step anyway and cover the area with overlapping sheets of cardboard. Old boxes from stores need opening out, their

Once raked over the bed can be planted. Mulch the surface with compost or manure twice a year, between harvests

Sellotape and staples removing, and weighting down along the edges with stones, poles and compost or soil. Put little or no organic matter on top, or the cardboard will rot too quickly.

After six weeks or so holes will appear in the cardboard with weeds poking through. Simply place another layer of cardboard on top.

All this can look a bit messy to start with, but the cardboard will soon either rot away or be covered by compost or well rotted manure.

By early June you will have clean soil ready to plant Brussels sprouts, leeks, runner beans, courgettes and tomatoes. Leave the cardboard in place – it makes excellent food for worms – just make holes and plant through it. At this point spread compost or manure over the cardboard.

Slug numbers should reduce after weeds have rotted and the mulching is finished. Using cardboard like this is usually needed only once.

Weed in the usual way from June onwards and there should be many less annual weeds than if the soil had been dug. Some perennials such as bindweed and couch grass will be weakened but not killed– if these are present lay down more cardboard in June. You can still grow vegetables through the cardboard, such as courgettes, pumpkins and brussels sprouts, but give them more space than usual.

CROSSWORD...

just for fun Answers below

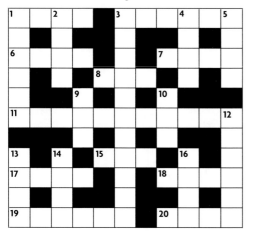

SPOT THE DIFFERENCE

If gloomy autumn and weather leaves you dreaming of next year's flower shows, here's a taste of what to look forward to next summer. But can you spot the FOUR differences between these two pictures?
(Answers can be found at the bottom of the page)

ACROSS

1 A grease _____ is placed around the trunk of fruit trees to trap certain pests (4)
3 Genus name for dogwood (6)
6 '____ Apple' is the old name for tomato (4)
7 Ms Swithinbank, the Gardeners' Question Time panellist (4)
8 Doctor found in wholesome whorls! (3)
11 Common name for Althaea officinalis, which grow in wetlands (11)
15 Finish, as in mending a tendril! (3)
17 Chrysanthemums that flower into November are called ____ chrysanths (4)
18 French town after which a strain of hybrid anemones is named (4)
19 Genus name for the silver wattle (6)
20 An excess of produce (4)

DOWN

1 Common name for a flower of the genus impatiens (6)
2 Dark blue, as in Agapanthus 'Wavy ____'! (4)
3 Genus name for the tamarillo, or New Zealand tomato (11)
4 Deriving from the Greek, this word is used in Latin plant names to denote that it is 'dwarf', eg. Berberis x stenophylla '____' (4)
5 A fertilized ovule, containing an embryonic plant; it usually comes in a packet with many others! (4)
9 Gardeners like to ___ the experts in a question and answer session (3)
10 Contracted virus, found in an influx of effluent! (3)
12 'Fruiting' tree of the juglans genus (6)
18 French town after which a strain of hybrid anemones is named (4)
13 Type of 'old fashioned' or shrub rose (4)
14 Genus of evergreen shrubs, including the so-called holly-leaved sweet spire (4)
16 Abnormal outgrowth from a plant's stem, leaf, flower or root, usually caused by insects, bacteria or fungi (4)

MINI GREENHOUSE, MINI PRICE!

THIS IS my wife Julie's mini bottle greenhouse which she made in the summer. It cost of £1 for the canes and £2 for silicone sealant. It measures 4ft by 3ft and is ideal for raising seedlings and young tomato plants.
Mr J Jozkow, Holyhead, Gwynedd

Problem solver

Q Raymond Pickles asks: "The top of my cordyline died but there are six nice green shoots at the base. What do I do with the 12ft (3.7m) or so of unsightly trunk?"

A Shorten the trunks to just above where shoots have formed. Do not seal the cuts. If a long spell of hard frost is predicted, cover new growth with fleece.

CROSSWORD ANSWERS **ACROSS** 3 Band 3 Cornus 6 Love 7 Anne 8 Who 11 Marshmallow 15 End 17 Late 18 Caen 19 Acacia 20 Glut **DOWN** 1 Balsam 2 Navy 3 Cyphomandra 4 Nana 5 Seed 9 Ask 10 Flu 12 Walnut 13 Alba 14 Itea 16 Gall
SPOT THE DIFFERENCE A sign is missing (bottom) and a plant label has been blanked out (centre). A chrysanth flower (centre) has changed from yellow to orange and a label has appeared (left).

Quick tips

November ...more things to do

① Insulate taps over winter

■ USE FOAM lagging to insulate all outdoor taps and pipework against freezing. If allowed to freeze, water within the tap or pipe will expand, causing splits or cracks, so the pipe will leak when it thaws.

② Guard woody plants

■ PLACE TREE guards or chicken wire around young trees and woody shrubs that are prone to attack from rabbits, deer and squirrels. This will stop them nibbling the bark which in turn could let diseases in.

③ Plant hardy pot-grown specimens

■ AS LONG as the ground is not frozen or waterlogged, keep planting out pot-grown hardy climbers, shrubs and trees. Remember to water through winter. It's also a good time to plant bare root specimens which are usually cheaper to buy.

④ Preventing wind rock

■ CUT BACK *Buddleja davidii* by half if the plant is tall and your garden is exposed, so putting it at risk from wind rock. These shrubs should be hard pruned properly in spring, to bring on new healthy growth.

⑤ Clean out bird boxes

■ NOW IS the optimum time to clean out bird nesting boxes. If you do not clean them out they can harbour wintering pests such as mites, as well as bird diseases. Remove old nesting material before scrubbing with clean water. Allow to dry and then dust with a wildlife-safe fungicide.

⑥ Final tulip planting

■ BY PLANTING tulips this late in autumn you'll have a better chance of preventing the bulbs being infected with the fungal disease tulip fire. But try to get them in soon. They are best in a lightly shaded spot that gets more sun as spring progresses.

⑦ Pruning grapevines

■ BEGIN PRUNING grapevines. Cut back all fruited shoots to one or two buds from the main stem. This can be carried out between now and late winter, but those under glass are best pruned early so that winter sunlight coming into the greenhouse is not blocked out.

DECEMBER 2013

SUNDAY

1

MONDAY

2

TUESDAY

3

WEDNESDAY

4

THURSDAY

5

FRIDAY

6

SATURDAY

7

SUNDAY

8

Grow your own mistletoe

Save berries from festive sprigs to sow on trees

I T IS possible to sow mistletoe on garden trees. Much of the mistletoe we buy at Christmas is harvested from apple trees in France. This is important as you'll have more chance of success if you sow your seeds on the same kind of tree as the mistletoe you bought. After the Christmas festivities, save berries in a plastic bag in cold (not freezing) conditions.

In March or early spring, select stout branches at least 3in (7.5cm) thick near the top of a well established apple tree. Make a nick in the bark with a sharp knife, squish the hard seed out of the centre of the mistletoe berry, and push it firmly into the nick.

Wind a strip of hessian around the branch once and tie it in place. Now wait two years to see it grow!

DECEMBER 2013

MONDAY

9

TUESDAY

10

WEDNESDAY

11

THURSDAY

12

FRIDAY

13

SATURDAY

14

SUNDAY

15

MONDAY

16

Make a simple cornus wreath

MAKING CHRISTMAS decorations from plant material is fun and rewarding. Here's a really easy one you can embellish with more bits if you want.

Prune some long, thin stems of red stemmed cornus – you could use willow or similar. They each need to be a little over 3ft (90cm) long. Take a bundle of three or four, line them up, twist the bundle and gently bend the stems until the ends cross. You need an overlap of about 4in (10cm) long tails.

Tie the point where they cross firmly together with strong twine. Now take thinner stems and twist them loosely around the loop, tying them in as necessary, or threading them between the thicker stems to lock in place.

Tie a pretty ribbon in a bow around the crossover point. We've added on a few dried chillies – you can make it as ornate as you like.

DECEMBER 2013

TUESDAY

17

WEDNESDAY

18

THURSDAY

19

FRIDAY

20

SATURDAY

21

SUNDAY

22

MONDAY

23

TUESDAY

24

Christmas veg cooking tips

Sprouts

■ Clean and roughly chop about 1lb of sprouts. Cut four rashers of bacon into pieces and dry fry until crispy. Remove the bacon and keep warm. Add the chopped sprouts to the pan, stir fry them in the bacon fat for a couple of minutes on a medium heat. Reduce the heat to very low, cover the pan and 'sweat' the sprouts for about 10 minutes, stirring occasionally, until cooked to your liking. When ready, stir in the bacon bits and serve.

Potatoes

■ Peel floury (usually maincrop) potatoes, then wash them and cut into quarters. Put them into a pan of boiling water and par-boil for about 10 minutes. Drain them thoroughly, put them back in the pan with a lid on it, and shake the pan until the edges of the potatoes are well roughed up. Heat a generous dollop of goose fat or dripping in a roasting tray, toss the potatoes in the fat then pop them into a pre-heated oven (200°C) until golden and crisp.

Carrots

■ Top and tail (you can leave a tuft of leaf stems on the top of each one for effect) then scrub some fresh, young carrots with a stiff veg brush or scouring pad. Place them in a pan with the zest and juice of an orange, put a lid on and simmer gently until tender, adding a splash of water if necessary. Drain, then toss in butter and drizzles with honey before serving.

DECEMBER 2013

WEDNESDAY
25

THURSDAY
26

FRIDAY
27

SATURDAY
28

SUNDAY
29

MONDAY
30

TUESDAY
31

More Christmas cooking tips

Enjoy red cabbage, sage and parsnips at their best

Red cabbage

■ Cut a red cabbage into quarters, cut out the woody stalk at the centre and finely shred the rest. Peel, core and finely chop a large Bramley cooking apple and one large onion, and cook them gently in a pan with some butter until tender. Add a good couple of twists of fresh nutmeg and four tablespoons of brown sugar, stir in the shredded cabbage and mix well. Put the mixture in a baking dish with a tight fitting lid, and cook in a low oven for about 2 hours.

Sage & onion stuffing

■ Chop an onion finely. Melt 2oz butter and gently fry the onion until softened. Stir in 4oz breadcrumbs and 2 tablespoons of freshly chopped sage. Season well. Tip into a baking dish, dot with butter, then bake in the oven at 180°C for about 30 minutes.

Parsnips

■ Top and tail, peel, quarter lengthways and cut the hard core out of the centre of each root. Simmer the pieces in boiling water for 5 minutes. Strain, and while still steaming toss the pieces in a 50:50 mix of seasoned grated Parmesan cheese and plain flour. Roast the coated pieces in hot fat until golden and crispy.

Anne Swithinbank is a regular panellist on *Gardeners' Question Time*

PET PLAYGROUND
For many years our greenhouse has had an important role to play as a dry winter run for our guinea pigs Nutkin (left) and Pumpkin

Anne Swithinbank

Cold comfort 'farm'

A couple of pet projects have been keeping **Anne** busy in the greenhouse

WORK IS focusing on the greenhouse at the moment, not least because the last two guinea pigs of our once-large herd need to move into their winter quarters. 'Herd' is the wrong collective noun for these popular pets, as it should be 'group'. I think a trundle or a scuttle sounds better – and that's exactly what they do, all over the greenhouse floor as they navigate their way between hutch, carrier and various pots and sacks of compost. Nutkin and Pumpkin live in the balmy, light and dry surroundings of the greenhouse by day and go back to a warmer stable at night.

Child's play

Gardens change as children arrive, grow up and move on, and I guess we're at the end stages of this. The first job here was to dig a run for our pet rabbits, which makes me laugh now. We soon gave up keeping rabbits, as we get regular visits from plenty of wild ones – and they don't need looking after!

I've never been able to plant up the expanse of lawn in the middle of the garden, as it has always been bagged for badminton, or as a football pitch.

As for pets, our collection reached its pinnacle when the children were at junior school, and it

> *"Our two remaining guinea pigs needed to move into warmer winter quarters"*

consisted of two rabbits, a hamster, fish, six guinea pigs, a budgie, nine bantams, a dog and about three ponies – though no more than two small ones ever lived on site. No wonder we rarely went away anywhere. All this, plus the occasional exercising of a dirt bike has taken its toll. But, one day, it will all be mine!

Winter beauties

Plonked on the greenhouse staging were two winter-flowering clematis (the evergreen *C. urophylla* 'Winter Beauty'), and as that is my headquarters, I took this as a hint that John wanted me to look after them. Although it is late, I'll plant them in good, well-cultivated soil where they'll put down roots before next spring and summer.

I don't have a suitable fence, so they'll have to scramble up deciduous shrubs, which means setting them to the outside of the twiggy growth so they can enjoy root space, light and air.

The fibrous-rooted, species-type clematis don't need the deeper planting meted out to larger-flowered hybrids, so I set them at a normal depth in the soil and spread a mulch of well-rotted compost over the roots. All I need to do is keep the weeds down and look forward to their showy white bells.

Step by step   Planting a winter-flowering clematis

ROOTS
After watering well or soaking, remove the pot and gently tease out roots to help them establish more quickly

SOIL
Plant them firmly, in good soil. Here I'm planting towards the edge of the *Euonymus alatus* in our front garden

TRAIN
A pea stick, pushed into the soil behind the clematis, will guide it towards the euonymus and other shrubs I want it to climb up

Ivy & the holly

Ivy Timmins is a shy, timid old lady, so will she find the courage to open her heart to the friendly villagers this Christmas? A short story by **Georgie Foord**

I**VY'S HOLLY** tree was the glory of the village. It towered above the garden wall, shielding the small, grey cottage behind it from prying eyes. Every autumn it bore great clusters of scarlet berries, set off to perfection by the glossy dark-green foliage. Visitors to the village would stop to gaze up at the tree, nod their heads knowingly and remark that a harsh winter was on the way. The residents, however, knew that the tree bestowed its bounty regardless of the weather forecast.

Ivy Timmins was born in the cottage more than 75 years ago. An only child, she grew up knowing that it would be her destiny to care for her parents as they grew older. She'd firmly suppressed any thoughts of marriage and family for herself, and appeared contented with her lot. After her mother passed on, the villagers regularly saw Miss Timmins pushing her ailing father round the lanes in his wheelchair, always stopping for a friendly word or two. The pair never missed the Sunday morning service at St Mark's.

But Ivy's serene little world fell apart when her years of caring for her father came to an abrupt end. She refused all offers of help, closed the door to visitors and ventured no further than the village shop for a her few meagre provisions. She stopped going to church, and forgot how to communicate with her neighbours. However Ivy's life was about to change.

It was the week before Christmas. The village shop displayed boxes of crackers, cards and rolls of shiny wrapping paper, and strung coloured lights around the shelves. Decorated Christmas trees appeared in cottage windows, and the local children, liberated from school, could scarcely contain their excitement.

Ivy would have been mortified to know that she was being discussed in the shop. "Poor soul," remarked Mrs Brady, resting her bulging shopping bag on the counter. "We ought to do something for her. She must be so lonely."

The vicar's wife was buying stamps at the post office counter. "You're quite right, Mrs B. It's such a shame. Leave it with me, and I'll see if John can come up with something."

Christmas meant little to Ivy. She had nobody to buy cards and presents for, no special meal to prepare, no desire to decorate the cottage. The holly tree in the garden provided all the festive cheer she needed...suddenly, she was startled by a knock at the front door.

Heart pounding, she peered from behind the curtain, and was horrified to see a young man standing on the step.

Before she could hide away he'd spotted her and gave a cheery wave, so Ivy cautiously opened the door a crack.

"Go away!" she snapped. "Whatever you're selling, I don't want any."

But he wasn't deterred. "Hello!" he smiled. "I'm not selling anything. I'm here to ask a favour."

He didn't look threatening, Ivy thought. And he wasn't wearing one of those 'hoodies' she'd read about. He continued: "My name's Paul. I'm the local scout leader. Look, here's my ID." He held the badge up for inspection.

Ivy sniffed and cautiously opened the door another inch, asking "Well? What do you want?"

"It's your beautiful holly tree. Hilltop Farm has no holly to spare this year and we – that is, the Scouts – were wondering if we might beg a few sprigs to decorate the church? We always help with the decorations at Christmas."

Ivy pursed her lips and made as if to shut the door. "My father loved that tree. It's never been cut. I leave it for the birds."

But Paul was nothing if not persuasive. "There'll be plenty for the birds, I promise you. And maybe it could do with a little pruning, after all these years?"

He paused, not wanting to push her too much. "The village would be very grateful if you could sacrifice – just a little."

Ivy had no experience of dealing with charming young men, but the female buried somewhere deep in her psyche slowly warmed to his friendly approach.

"Oh, very well. I suppose the birds can spare a few berries this year."

He took her small, chilly hands in his large, warm grasp. "Bless you, Miss Timmins. You're so kind."

He paused at the gate on his way out, his gaze taking in the neglected garden. A sea of rank, dun-coloured grass and weeds encroached on the cottage from all sides. The holly tree was the one brilliant splash of seasonal colour in an otherwise depressing garden.

Seeing his expression, Ivy shrugged "I know, it's a mess. My father was a great gardener. His roses were the talk of the village – before you were born young man. But it's all too much for me. I wouldn't know where to start." She closed the door.

On Christmas morning Paul returned once more, knocking on Ivy's door. "Get your best hat," he said. "I'm taking you to church."

She gasped. "Oh no. I couldn't, Paul. Really, I'd feel so awkward after all this time."

"No excuses. You need to come and see what we've done with your holly. And there's coffee and mince pies in the hall when the service is finished."

Ivy realised she'd grown, perhaps, just a little fond of this young man. "In a different life," she thought, "I could have had a grandson like him." She allowed herself to be persuaded.

St Mark's looked magnificent, awash with arrangements of white lilies, hellebores and chrysanthemums. Ivy's holly branches were ranged along the windowsills, shining in the pale winter sunlight. "Father would be so pleased," she thought.

The Vicar's sermon ended with a special plea: "My friends, we are all being encouraged to do our bit for the environment. I know that many of you would like to grow vegetables for your families, but your gardens are too small. I wonder, do any of you have spare land you would be willing to let others cultivate?"

"Why is he looking at me?" Ivy wondered. Then the penny dropped. She turned to Paul. "They could have my garden," she whispered.

Paul exchanged a glance with the Vicar in the pulpit. Ivy's neglected plot will be put to good use. She'll make new friends, and become part of village life again.

Mission accomplished!

Your gardening week

Ornamental garden

Caring for poinsettias

Try our tips to keep this classic Christmas houseplant looking good for months

Poinsettias are now available in classy whites or pinks, as well as traditional red. All need the same care

THOUGH THEY'RE often thrown away when they lose their colour, poinsettias actually make a rather stunning houseplant with their green, shapely leaves in the summer. And it is possible to get the plant to turn itself back into the Christmas beauty we love from November onwards.

Poinsettias are what is known as short day length plants – plants, which 'flower' when the days are short and night time is long.

On a commercial scale flowering is forced in glasshouses that are blacked out for long periods, but it is possible to do this at home (see the Care through the year panel).

Poinsettias have a sap that can irritate the skin and eyes, so always wear gloves when handling them.

Poinsettias may die after a few weeks in the home through no fault of the owner. This is usually down to bad handling before the plants are delivered to the retailer. British grown plants will have been less stressed, so buy UK-grown poinsettias wherever possible.

QUICK TIP

When leaves fall from your poinsettia, clear them promptly so they do not harbour diseases

Feeding

■ A MONTHLY FEED is best, using a high potash fertilizer such as Tomato food. Feeding is more important when the plant is putting on new growth in summer. For ease over Christmas, try a specialist drip feed such as Vitax Poinsettia and Christmas cacti liquid plant food. It will give a controlled feed over 30 days.

Care over Christmas

■ Provide bright, filtered light over the Christmas period

■ **Keep away from strong direct light as this can scorch the leaves**

■ Poinsettias do not like cold draughty places, so keep away from doors

■ **Keep the temperature above 13°C (55°F) Preferably around 18°C (64°F)**

Watering

■ ONLY WATER when the surface of the compost has begun to dry out. However poinsettias like high humidity around foliage, so mist regularly to extended the flowering period over Christmas.

After Christmas

■ Reduce watering through Feb- March. In April prune plants back to 4in(10cm).
In early May move plants to a south-facing windowsill.
Take softwood cuttings if needed in May, but remember to wear gloves.
When new shoots appear, repot using JohnInnes No3 with added grit.
Keep temperature at 60-65°F (15-18°c).
In November, stimulate flowering by first giving the plant maximum daylight for a few days, then placing it in a dark room or cover loosely with a black plastic bag.

Your gardening week
Kitchen garden

Make a bird nesting box

How to make a simple, low cost bird box ahead of the breeding season

PUTTING UP A BIRD box now means potential occupants will have time to get used to it ahead of the breeding season. This one-plank system is a tried and tested method – it's probably been around for generations.

While some of the cutting and nailing can be challenging for young children, with a bit of parental or grandparental help, this is a simple and fun project to occupy an afternoon for any kids feeling the boredom factor this half term. Get hold of a 6in (15cm) wide plank – you may even have one already knocking around in the shed or garage – mark out the shapes in the illustration (2.5cm = 1in) and get building:

Tools and Equipment

- Tape measure
- Pencil
- Drill
- Spade bit for entrance
- Wood saw
- Hammer
- Mitre square
- Nails/panel pins
- Tacks
- Waterproof material for roof hinge
- Netting staples

| Backboard | Base | Side | ◯ | Side | Roof | Front |
| 53cm | 10.5cm | 25cm | | 20cm | 21.5cm | 20cm |

1 ■ Measure then mark up your plank as illustrated. Use a saw to cut out all the pieces, remembering to make an angled cut between the roof and front panel to match the angle of the sides. Smooth rough edges with sand paper and use the drill bit to make the entrance hole (inset).

2 ■ Nail the pieces together, having first played with them to get an idea of how they fit. It is easier to start the first few nails off on a firm surface (inset) before nailing the first two parts together. Start by attaching the two side panels to the base. The backboard should then be attached, followed by the front.

3 ■ Attach the roof. Nests should be cleared out in autumn, so the roof needs to be hinged. To keep the box weatherproof this needs to be a single piece of rubber material firmly tacked to the roof and backboard – pieces of tyre inner tube or pond liner are ideal. Hammer a netting staple to both the roof and side panel (inset). Wire these together to secure the roof.

4 ■ Hang your box. Place at least 5ft (1.5m) from the ground. The entrance should face away from prevailing winds and direct sunlight – an aspect between north and south east is best. Position it away from bird feeding areas. Use screws, nails or wire to fix in place. It can often take a few seasons before the box is used.

SIZE MATTERS
This bird box will accommodate birds little bigger than a sparrow, but the size of the entrance hole will determine which bird species will seek to occupy your box.

HOLE SIZE	SPECIES
25 mm	Blue Tits, Marsh Tits, and Coal Tits
28 mm	Great Tits, Pied Flycatcher and Tree Sparrow
32 mm	House Sparrows and Nuthatches

Quick tips

December ...more things to do

1 Sowing alpines

■ IN THE WILD, alpine seeds have to go through a period of cold weather before they germinate. Copy this at home by sowing the seeds now in a pot and standing it outdoors; the seeds will periodically freeze and thaw, so breaking their dormancy. They will germinate in spring- pot on when big enough.

2 Cosy compost

■ COVER YOUR COMPOST heap with old carpet or black plastic sheeting to keep the temperature up so decomposition can continue in the cold. Keep turning if possible and watch out for any animal life that may become trapped by your insulating layer.

3 Clean paths

■ CLEAR PATHS OF LICHEN, moss, weeds and other plant debris to minimize the risk of slipping in wet or icy conditions. On a dry day, clear as much as possible by hand, using a narrow-bladed trowel or bulb planter before applying an outdoor-specific surface cleaner such as Westland Patio and Decking Hero. This will prevent problems re-appearing quickly.

4 Be prepared!

■ STORE AT LEAST one bag of sowing compost, one potting-on compost and one multi-purpose now in warm dry conditions. When needed quickly it will not be frozen or waterlogged, which can't be said of the bags stored outside by garden centres. Plants and seeds do not do well in sodden, cold compost.

5 Root cuttings

■ THERE IS STILL TIME to take root cuttings from dormant plants such as Celastrus 'Bittersweet' and Chaenomeles' japonica. Wash and remove a section of pencil-thickness root; cut at an angle at the base; straight cut at the top. Plant in damp cutting compost.

6 Planting raspberry canes

■ AS LONG as the ground is not frozen or waterlogged, you can plant out raspberry canes. Prepare the site by digging in well-rotted manure. Spread out roots in a wide planting hole, setting canes to the soil mark on the stem. Space canes at 14-16in (40-45cm) apart.

7 Save plastic bottles

■ POT ON ANY SUMMER cuttings that have taken well, showing root growth through the base and healthy top growth. If planting into the ground, the soil is still warm enough to encourage roots to take. And if potting into a pot one size larger, there is still time for the plants to settle before temperatures fall.